John A. Williams

Twayne's United States Authors Series

Warren French, Editor

Indiana University, Indianapolis

TUSAS 472

JOHN A. WILLIAMS
(1925–   )
Photograph by Craig E. Blair

John A. Williams

By Gilbert H. Muller

LaGuardia Community College
City University of New York

Twayne Publishers • Boston

John A. Williams

Gilbert H. Muller

Copyright © 1984 by G. K. Hall & Company
All Rights Reserved
Published by Twayne Publishers
A Division of G. K. Hall & Company
70 Lincoln Street
Boston, Massachusetts 02111

Book Production by John Amburg

Book Design by Barbara Anderson

Printed on permanent/durable acid-free
paper and bound in the United States of
America.

**Library of Congress Cataloging in
Publication Data**

Muller, Gilbert H.
 John A. Williams.

 (Twayne's United States authors series ; TUSAS 472)
 Bibliography: p. 163
 Includes index.
 1. Williams, John Alfred, 1925-
--Criticism and interpretation.
 2. Afro-Americans in literature.
 I. Title. II. Series.
PS3573.I4495Z8 1984   813'.54   83-26541
ISBN 0-8057-7413-0

Contents

About the Author

Gilbert H. Muller was born in Brooklyn, New York in 1941. He received his BA from the University of Kentucky in 1953; his MA from Stanford University in 1966; and his PhD in English and American Literature from Stanford in 1967. Currently Professor of English at the LaGuardia campus of the City University of New York, he has also taught at Shiraz University and Damavand College in Iran, and at Stanford University.

Muller is the author of *Nightmares and Visions: Flannery O'Connor and the Catholic Grotesque* (1972), which won the Parks Award for the best study of southern fiction and was listed as one of the outstanding works in criticism in 1973 by the Association of College and Research Libraries. His essays and reviews have appeared in the *New York Times*, the *New Republic*, the *Nation*, the *New Leader*, *Newsday*, the *Sewanee Review*, the *Georgia Review*, *Studies in Short Fiction*, *Renascence*, and elsewhere. He is also a noted author of textbooks in English and composition, including *The Basic English Handbook*, *The Short Prose Reader* (with Harvey Wiener), and *The McGraw-Hill Reader*.

Among Muller's awards are a National Endowment for the Humanities Fellowship, a Fulbright Fellowship, a Mellon Fellowship, a National Endowment for the Humanities summer seminar grant, and City University of New York Faculty Research Fellowships.

Preface

Nowhere is the richness and variety of contemporary American literature more evident than in the work of John Alfred Williams. Born in 1925, Williams has been exploring the myths and realities of the black experience—and, unavoidably, the American experience—for more than three decades. As novelist, biographer, historian, autobiographer, anthologist, editor, and journalist, he is a unique writer who has attempted to investigate how all of black America fits into the national and international jigsaw puzzle. His varied career, his intellectual range, and the caliber of his best writing make him a significant figure in modern American letters.

Although Williams has published more than a dozen books and scores of articles, he has not received extensive critical recognition. There is considerable evidence that he has had to fight his way out of the literary ghetto to which many talented black American writers have been consigned and that his progress as an artist has not been easy. The retraction of his American Academy of Arts and Letters fellowship by the American Academy in Rome in 1962—an event analyzed by Williams in *The Man Who Cried I Am* and in his essay, "We Regret to Inform You That"—is one of the most disquieting episodes in recent American literary history. Moreover, as early as 1967, Eliot Fremont-Smith, in a *New York Times* review, noted that Williams "is an excellent writer who has been unlucky. He has been justly compared with Ralph Ellison and James Baldwin but his books have come earlier." Williams's books, of course, did not come earlier, but Fremont-Smith was correct in his basic assertion that Williams's lack of literary luck was due to race and racism. Nevertheless, Williams managed to make his way as a writer in America. He kept the faith, and younger writers, as Ishmael Reed has observed, look to Williams instead of

Baldwin or Ellison, seeing in him the true link between earlier black writers and the artists of the current generation.

Williams's life and his journey as an artist in America constitute the first chapter in this study; it presents new material based on interviews with Williams, letters, and unpublished sketches. The many facets of Williams's life—his education, his numerous jobs, his term in the Navy, his two marriages, his extensive travels—illuminate the lives of characters in his fiction. Because the autobiographical impulse in Williams's fiction is strong, this initial chapter on his life will help readers to understand his evolution as a writer. Like several of his major characters, Williams has been driven by the need to succeed. He is the primary chronicler of the black American middle class, specifically of people who, like himself, wrestle with the American dream in their invariably painful attempts to discover their true country.

Another key influence on Williams's fiction has been his career as a journalist, nonfiction author, and freelance writer. Chapter 2 traces some of the themes and concerns in his essays and nonfiction works that influence his fiction. Many of the essays Williams has published over more than thirty years have been collected in *Flashbacks*, one of his best and most important books. He has also written two books for young audiences (*Africa: Her History, Land, and People* and *The Most Native of Sons*); a highly critical study of Martin Luther King, Jr. (*The King God Didn't Save*); and a fine autobiographical odyssey (*This is My Country Too*), a black man's answer to Steinbeck's *Travels With Charley*. Recurring subjects, themes, and motifs in the nonfiction—the sociology of black culture, history and politics, the artist in America, exile and return, the American dream, among others—are those that form Williams's central vision as a writer of fiction.

Williams's reputation as a major American writer rests on his fiction, and the major part of this study offers a careful analysis and evaluation of his nine novels, examining the evolution of his art and ideas through three main stages. The initial stage, analyzed in chapter 3, embraces Williams's first three novels—*One for New York* (1960), *Night Song* (1961), and *Sissie* (1963). These semiautobiographical novels, which constitute the author's early fiction, are increasingly original in subject matter, progressively more daring in execution, moving toward the self-assurance seen in *Sissie*. (David Boroff in the *Saturday Review* observes: "Where *Another Country* is shrill and noisy, *Sissie* is permeated by a quiet anger that builds and builds inexorably.") These three novels concentrate on the American dream and on its contradictions. *Sissie*, the notable novel of this early period, is not a "rags to riches" testament, but rather the chronicle of black life in transition; in it, as in Williams's earlier novels, the author attempts to find alternatives to racial violence in America. This vision of solutions without violence is central to the first major phase in John Williams's career as a novelist.

A gap of four years occurred between the publication of *Sissie* and the release of Williams's next novel, *The Man Who Cried I Am*. Williams had been shocked by the American Academy in Rome episode and preoccupied by the increasing violence, racial polarization, and cultural and political breakdown of the 1960s. *The Man Who Cried I Am* is the most important political novel of the decade, and central to the second stage of his career. The other two novels that round out this second phase are *Sons of Darkness, Sons of Light* (1969), and *Captain Blackman* (1972). These three novels trace America's increasing paralysis during the 1960s, focusing on political assassinations, urban conflagrations, the Vietnam War—a general societal malaise set against the larger backdrop of national and world history. They amount to a trilogy of political novels, somewhat reminiscent of *U.S.A.* (Dos Passos is one of the few writers to whom Williams will acknowledge a literary debt), that offer a trenchant and troubled assessment of American political history.

The third stage in Williams's evolution as a novelist is still in certain ways in progress. Two novels definitely belong to this third phase. One is *Mothersill and the Foxes* (1975), a parody of black sexuality in which the major character is put through bizarre stations of an erotic Cross—incest, satyriasis, voyeurism, compulsive masturbation—only to move toward final absolution. The second is *The Junior Bachelor Society* (1976), a remarkable synthesis of vision and technical virtuosity, a novel that takes the lives of nine black men and projects them as emblems of survival in a fierce and constantly repressive world. Although there is violence in these two novels, it is peripheral to Williams's key concerns. Williams withholds hecatombs in the books, seeking instead resolutions that come from battles fought and won "within the system." In both novels, there is a tentative spirit of affirmation, achieved at a cost, but leaving men and women intact.

A similar tone prevails in *!Click Song* (1982), but this brilliant novel also taps the strengths revealed in the political fiction of his second phase. Thus Williams attempts to consolidate his art, and also to explore new directions, including work in poetry, drama, nonfiction, and assuredly, the novel. John Williams is an artist, as he would say, of some probability. He knows the ugliness and potential beauty in the American grain, and he writes about it persuasively. He is an important and distinctive American writer.

Gilbert H. Muller

LaGuardia Community College
City University of New York

Acknowledgments

I should like to thank John Williams for his graciousness and unfailing good humor in responding to my queries, submitting autobiographical material, and making himself available for interviews. I am also grateful for his permission to quote material from his works.

I am pleased to acknowledge support from the National Endowment for the Humanities, the Mellon Foundation, and the City University of New York that enabled me to concentrate on the development of the study.

Finally, it is a pleasure to acknowledge the help of Warren French, who encouraged and supported this study from the outset to its completion.

Chronology

1925   John Alfred Williams born December 5 near Jackson, Mississippi, oldest of four children.

1925-1943   Grows up in the Fifteenth Ward, Syracuse, New York. Attends Washington Irving Elementary, Madison Junior High, and Central High School.

1943   Joins the Navy, serving in the Pacific; receives honorable discharge in 1946.

1946   Completes high school and enrolls at Syracuse University.

1947   Marries first wife, Carolyn Clopton. First son Gregory born, 1948.

1950   Receives BA in June from Syracuse University; enters Graduate School.

1951   Works in foundry, clerks in supermarket. Second son Dennis born.

1952   Caseworker at the Onondaga County Welfare Department.

1954   Leaves in summer for California. Works for Golden State Mutual Life Insurance, for CBS, and for NBC TV publicity special events. Moves to New York City.

1955   Staff member for special events programs at Columbia Broadcasting System in New York. Publicity director for Comet Press Books. First and second drafts of *The Angry Ones.*

1956   Edits and publishes *Negro Market Newsletter.*

1957   Divorced. Assistant to publisher at Abelard-Schuman. Director of Information for American Committee on Africa.

1958   Correspondent for *Ebony* and *Jet* in Europe, also for National Negro Press Association.

1959   Fund raiser for National Committee for a Sane Nuclear Policy.

1960   *The Angry Ones* (*One for New York*).

1961   *Night Song.*

1962   *Africa: Her History, Lands and People.* Edits the *Angry Black.* Nomination for the Prix de Rome rejected by the American Academy in Rome.

1963   *Sissie.* Travels across the United States on assignment for *Holiday.*

1964   *The Protectors.* Travels in Africa, Europe, Israel, and Cyprus.

1965   Marries Lorrain Isaac. Travels in Africa for *Newsweek. This Is My Country Too.* Writes and narrates TV film, "Omowale, The Child Returns Home."

1967   *The Man Who Cried I Am.* Lecturer in writing at City College of New York.

1968   Guest lecturer at the College of the Virgin Islands. Son Adam born.

1969   *Sons of Darkness, Sons of Light.*

1970   *The Most Native of Sons. The King God Didn't Save.* Edits *Amistad 1.*

1971   Edits *Amistad 2.* First visit to Grenada, West Indies.

1972   *Captain Blackman.* Second visit to Grenada.

1973   *Flashbacks.*

1973   Distinguished Professor at City University of New York (until 1977).

1975   *Mothersill and the Foxes. Minorities in the City.*

1976   *The Junior Bachelor Society.*

1978-1979   Visiting Professor at Boston University.

1979   Professor of English at Rutgers University (Newark) (through present).

1980   Returns to Grenada under new government. Visits Kenya for first time.

1981   Television adaptation of *The Junior Bachelor Society.*

1982   *!Click Song.*

Chapter One

John Williams:
An American Odyssey

Born on December 5, 1925 in Hinds County, Mississippi, close to the city of Jackson, John Alfred Williams grew up to become, as he once observed whimsically, a writer by accident. If not for job dissatisfaction, an evolving consciousness of the ways that race defines the contours of the American experience, and a desire to be an artist in America, Williams might have remained a foundry worker, a supermarket clerk, a butler, a caseworker, an insurance salesman—any one position in the constellation of jobs he held prior to his thirtieth year. In 1954, however, following a depressing year in California where he had worked as an agent for Golden State Mutual Life, Williams asked himself a fundamental question: Where had he come from, and where was he going? Who was this son of a son of a son of a son of a slave—Mandingo, Krie, Baule? He had come out of fog, he would tell himself later, but not to perish in it. Thus John Williams began "the process of becoming a writer," not for money or fame, but "to keep my sanity and find some purpose in life."[1] He would create himself and the world anew, striving persistently to define himself and the essence of American life through art.

Although Williams concentrates on the black American experience in his work, the true dimensions of his art are much broader than race and ethnicity. In fact, one of John Williams's great strengths is that he straddles polymorphous worlds and cultures more successfully than most contemporary writers. There is a problem in critical interpretation and assessment here that Saunders Redding elucidates when, speaking of black American writing, he observes that it "is fed by the same roots sunk in the same cultural soil as writing by white Americans. Nevertheless, both academic and popular criticism has exaggerated the distinction into a dichotomy that has been the source of grave critical injustice to Negro writing on the one hand and that—until recently at any rate—tended to vitiate its effectiveness as an instrument of social and cultural diagnosis and as a body of American experience through which we are enabled to understand the cultural psychology of the American world and, indeed—I think—the whole Western world."[2] Of course, it is still critically fashionable to define American writers by race, sex, ethnicity, region, or religion. Yet ultimately, any significant writer's stature rests on more absolute criteria than accidental matters of birth, origin, and affiliation, even as these attributes can nurture and support the development of the artist. John Williams starts typically with race in his work but he is at his greatest when assessing the pulse of a people and a nation—indeed the entire modern world—evolving through a series of historical conflicts.

John Williams is a tenacious explorer of the American landscape and of the Western world, ranging close in and far out in his fiction and nonfiction to measure the modern condition. He does not trap himelf in the web of words or in involuted structures that characterize postmodernist fiction. He attempts to communicate his vision in more conventional narrative forms, some of which are complex in themselves but comprehensible. Working typically with what he knows intimately—with felt life that often contains autobiographical elements and overtones—John Williams traces in his art a unique odyssey. This journey, embarked upon as much by the author as by his characters, embraces all periods of American history and assumes, finally, the whole world as its margins.

Origins

Following a long-standing tradition of the Williams family to return to its origins for childbirth, Ola Williams and her husband traveled to Mississippi in 1925 for the delivery of their first child. John Williams had been conceived ("with gusto, I hope," he declares in an undated and unpublished autobiographical essay) in Syracuse, New York, a city that had had a black population since 1769; Syracuse would define his life from 1925 to 1953 and beyond. While the South would not figure prominently in his work, his consciousness of the fact that he is a northerner born out of the immediacy of the southern past contributes to the totality of Williams's vision and the range of his landscapes. Moreover, he declares that his parents' trip South for his birth created a congenital impulse in him to travel. "That journey to Mississippi in 1925 and the return to Syracuse still represent the longest trip my father has ever made. That trip, plus the memory of the trains that rolled down the street near our house, must have triggered something in me; I've crossed America five times and visited twenty-eight countries, some of them two or three times. The lust for travel could have started in the womb."[3]

Ola Williams was 20 when she gave birth to John, the first of four children. Her husband, John Henry Williams, was 23. Ola herself was the eldest in a family of three boys and five girls from a farm family in Hinds County. She received her education at Tougaloo College outside Jackson, Mississippi. According to Williams, Tougaloo in those days was merely a domestic training school where his mother learned to cook, clean, and keep things generally tidy according to the tastes not of her family, but of white people. "Finished with the course," he indicates in an unpublished 1978 sketch, "she was then more or less indentured off to a good Christian family in the north—Syracuse in fact, and that is where she met my father." Traveling south to join his wife for the delivery, dressed in the starched white shirts that the author recalls as his father's identity tag, John Henry Williams discovered that white people did not take kindly to black men wearing white shirts if it was not Sunday. Even Joseph Jones, Ola's father, was bewildered by this strange deportment, determining not to like his son-in-law and labeling him shiftless.

The Mississippi police also were suspicious of this northern black man with his defiant white shirts, and when a

minor crime occurred in the area, the farm of John
Williams's grandfather was visited by the law. Williams's
mother recalls that the sheriff asked, "Joe, some niggers
done so and so, and your son-in-law's the only strange nigger around, so it must have been him. Where's he at?" Pro-
tected by his in-laws, John Henry Williams escaped immediately in a passing haywagon, which was stopped at one
point by the police. The police did not bother to pull out the
hay; they stuck pitchforks in it instead. Williams's father got
a tine in his shoulder, but managed to keep quiet, thereby
escaping. Within the year, Ola, with her son John, rejoined
her husband in Syracuse.

Williams writes, "I learned my America in Syracuse, New
York, a city that came into existence because of the great salt
beds beneath its foundations."[4] He asserts that he did not
have a bad childhood, despite the Depression years. In fact,
his boyhood in Syracuse was suffused with both pastoral
delights and gentle urban rhythms:

For me, Syracuse was my home and I knew it as such; its hills and
creeks; its lakes; its alleys; its parks. I knew what the roads felt like
after a hot day—soft, so soft you could sink into the asphalt deeper
than the sole of your shoe. I knew the winters, when snow came
for days on end and rose so high that you had to stand on the porch
to see across the street. Church picnics and near drownings I
remember, and scooters made from two-by-fours, roller skates and
crates, and rubber guns triggered with clothespins, and homes
with kitchens as large as the living room I now have. I remember
my father playing touch football in the roadway when work was
slow, and the slap of men's shoes as they raced down the street
grunting and shouting for a pass: "I'm in the clear, Stosh!" Black
men and white men, little men and big men.[5]

John Williams had a childhood defined only partially by
the Depression, which impinged of course on virtually all
American families. Nor was he a victim of that curious "double consciousness" which W. E. B. DuBois declared in *The
Souls of Black Folk* as the psychological hallmark of black
Americans. Williams would develop this dual perception in
due course; but according to him, blacks in Syracuse during
the Depression did not consider themselves unusual victims

of any "special set of circumstances." If blacks were unemployed, there were even more whites who experienced the same condition.

Syracuse for Williams during his childhood was a world defined by the melting pot atmosphere of the Fifteenth Ward. He started kindergarten at Washington Irving Elementary School, between Madison and Harrison Streets. In grade school, he was a good student, except in arithmetic.[6] He fell in love with Miss Lloyd, his fifth-grade teacher. He played the water whistle and triangle at a couple of ice cream socials. Next to playing ball, he enjoyed reading indiscriminately. "Just any goddam thing that came my way. The *Shadow* magazines, all pulp mags, *Boy's Life*, *The Rover Boys*, *Tom Swift*, *Tarzan* (and anything else by Burroughs) and all kinds of sports books."[7] Outside school, Williams went to the city-sponsored events in Thornden Park, delighting in the smell of cut grass and buttered popcorn. He participated in the NRA parades after Roosevelt was elected, riding in the back of a truck with other children, all dressed in striped cellophane costumes to symbolize that they were busy bees for the Administration. He went to the Dunbar Center and the Boy's Club, learning to swim, play pool and basketball, to fight, to read ("I must have been the greatest book thief ever to enter the Boy's Club library," he declares in a January 5, 1979 letter), to think, reason, win, and lose. He fell in love serially, but always with girls who did not love him. Rejected at Post Office and other petting games, Williams yearned to get into real trouble—to get caught at a craps game or stealing cans of tuna fish or candy bars. He wanted to be injured riding on the backs of trucks in winter, but he never was. He was confident—and lucky.

There were also more somber days during the Depression, days Williams says were "filled with shame and sullenness about being on welfare or relief. My brother and my two sisters were younger; they didn't know what was going on. I hated to wear the clothes; hated to go to the center to pick up the food; hated to carry home the loaves of bread with their white, waxed paper that told everyone you were on welfare. Hated it. But could do nothing about it."[8] Williams would embody the tonalities of life in Syracuse during the

Depression in several of his novels, notably *Sissie* and *The Junior Bachelor Society*. In the family of the Joplins, first presented in *Sissie* and subsequently in *The Man Who Cried I Am*, *The Junior Bachelor Society*, and *!Click Song*, he would locate an archetypal domestic grouping in his fiction that is based to an extent on the history of the Williams family. In a very real sense, both John Williams and the Joplins have been shaped by their origins in Syracuse's Fifteenth Ward.

Jew Town, the Fifteenth Ward was called, largely because of the Jewish businesses in the area—Sunny Simon's Saloon, Saslow's Fish Market, Bloom's Bakery, Berman's Ice and Coal Yard, Volinsky's Bakery, Simon's Texaco Garage. It was actually a polyglot world composed of East European, black American, Italian, Irish, German, and Anglo families. The four-unit house that the Williamses lived in contained black, Jewish, and Italian families, and was typical of the shared experiences and integrated nature of the Fifteenth Ward. When people lost jobs and savings ran out, there were always communal remedies. "When the Depression finally hit," notes Williams, "a lot of us were forced to live 'on the book,' on credit. Mrs. Levy, next door to us, had a stove in the front of her house and lived in back with her sons, Miltie and Hermie. Mrs. Levy gave credit, laboriously writing down the items sold and the cost. Not with a good heart mind you, but with the sullennness of someone caught in a trap. But when the bill was paid at the end of a week or two, she smiled and even gave us B-B bat suckers."[9]

Four blocks to the east of Washington Irving Grammar School was Madison Junior High, and it was here, as a teenager, that Williams's perception of life began to alter. For one thing, despite his adolescent pranks and average grades, Williams had perceptible talent. One day while the boy was fooling around with his buddies, his exasperated English and French teacher, Doris Schamu, a tiny woman, grabbed John and said, "John Williams, you're not like those other boys. You're not like them!" Mixed with the talent, perhaps a concomitant of it, was Williams's growing perception that shadows were developing over the placidity and pleasures of youth. "Only when I was a teenager," he has written, "did the dream of America begin to taste sour in my mouth. I was not a good student, nor was I a bad one. There was a period when I would be in school for a time, then out of it to help out. I was the first-born of four. At a time when the white boys I knew were still going to school, I was riding sanitation department trucks, emptying steel barrels filled with ashes. Even some of my black friends had not left school. I spent my evenings dripping bitterness and trying to take extra classes at night to catch up."[11] This itinerant's role, with Williams trying to get an education (and later trying to write) while holding a variety of jobs, would become a constant pattern in his life. But at Central High School, faced with job responsibilities and confused by the recent separation of his parents, Williams found a certain discipline and a pocket of repose in sports. "Pat Kane was the football coach," Williams recalls. "He kicked ass in an Irish way. Ed Friedlander was the track coach, and he kicked ass in a German way. Ed Brosco, from Notre Dame. But I found a great deal of discipline with those guys and sense of belonging—that is, an extension of belonging for I did belong to gangs—that was unlike the sense I'd had before. This belonging seemed to open out on the world within our greatly mixed teams." In one of the best evocations of the sports mystique in American fiction, Williams in *The Junior Bachelor Society* would pay homage to the competitors and teammates in the Fifteenth Ward, all of whom in curious elliptical ways reaffirm the tenacity of the American dream.

The Voyage Outward

Still, the very struggle, as Williams terms it, to keep his original dream of America alive was exhausting. On December 7, 1941, only two days past his sixteenth birthday, on leave from Central High School while working for the Hi-Speed Messenger Service, John Williams learned of Pearl Harbor. The war seemed to offer a necessary change for him, an alternative to the broken home life, the pressures of combining school and biking packages all over the city. Williams joined the Navy on April 8, 1943, leaving high school to be completed after the war. Trained as a hospital corpsman at the segregated naval base at Great Lakes, he was part of the first class of black Americans admitted to the rank. Williams was sent overseas early in 1944 and served with the Seventeenth Special Naval Construction Battalion, which was attached to the Fourth and then the First Marine Divisions. His tour covered New Caledonia, New Hebrides, the Solomons, the Marshalls, the Palau group, and the Marianas.

Finding himself for the first time beyond the relatively integrated and secure world of the Fifteenth Ward, Williams was exposed while in the Navy to both crude and subtle manifestations of racism:

I saw white Marines and black sailors line up for a race riot on Guam. A Chamorro girl told me she had been warned to stay away from black men because they had tails. My parents wrote asking what was being cut out of my letters; I had endless conferences with the censors and refused to stop writing home and saying the Navy was rotten. I have a pitted face from the dry shaves I got in the Marine brig. I traveled up and down the islands of the Pacific because black hospital corpsmen were not wanted aboard ship, and I wound up with a land force. A white Texan on a dark night in the New Hebrides was a minute away from shooting me. A white Mississippian who had been there and who had dissuaded the Texan told me, "Williams, you ain't like them other niggers." When I told him he was wrong, he laughed. "*You* crazy," he said "They ain't."[12]

Nothing in the fifteenth Ward, which was something of a racial and ethnic oasis, had prepared Williams for the virulence of racism in the Navy. Writing home to his mother in an undated letter shortly after the Japanese surrender, Williams concludes: "I'm not overly happy and neither is anyone else and I can guess the reason why. Everyone is thinking about the coming fight ahead. I mean the fight to be equal to any damn body else in the world."

Williams's experience in the Navy between 1943 and his discharge on January 4, 1946, would serve as a catalyst in his fiction. His first novel, started in the early 1950s, was an aborted attempt to deal with racism in the military. One of his few short stories, "Navy Black," is part of this planned but abandoned novel. This story is close to the author's actual experience of World War II. It is a subtle account of racial pressures that prevent a black cook stationed with the twenty-seventh Special Naval Construction Battalion on Micronesia from adopting a Chamorro boy. A three-part story, "Navy Black" is set on the day that the atomic bomb was dropped on Hiroshima. A complex rendition of multiple varieties of racism—white, black, Micronesian, and Japanese—the story explores the ambiguities inherent in black Americans fighting overseas for their country. Years later, Williams would develop this theme fully in *Captain Blackman*, a novel that is a product of his mature phase and one that offers an epic account of racism in the American military.

Upon discharge, Williams returned to Syracuse to finish high school in the spring of 1946, then went south to Morris Brown College in Atlanta to play football. This southern exposure, however, was brief. Not liking the region, Williams left the day classes were to begin, taking the Jim Crow train back to Syracuse where, under the GI Bill, he enrolled at Syracuse University. During his undergraduate days, Williams worked most semesters as a hospital orderly. Moreover, with a growing interest in writing and majoring in journalism, Williams began contributing pieces to the black press—the Syracuse Progressive *Herald*, the Chicago *Defender*, the National Negro Press Association. Williams wrote about anything assigned to him: visiting black and white bands; speeches by black clergymen; Syracuse sports events, notably involving the International Baseball League, which had Jackie Robinson coming to town with the Montreal Royals to play the Syracuse Chiefs. His articles appeared without by-line. Adding to the pressures of college, part-time work, and writing was Williams's marriage in 1947 to Carolyn Clopton and the birth of his first son, Gregory, in 1948. Williams graduated from Syracuse in June 1950 and went to graduate school the following summer. He broke off to take a job in the fall, planning to return to college the next year, an expectation never fulfilled.

Williams was not making much money writing in the late 1940s and early 1950s, but he persisted with his journalism, even when *Ebony* turned him down for a job in the winter of 1951. (Its publisher, John H. Johnson, admonished Williams to imitate Dan Burley of the *Amsterdam News* rather than try to develop a personal style.) The 1950s were apprentice years for Williams, involving writing, job seeking, and job switching—all placing strains on his marriage. His family had expanded with the birth of a second son, Dennis, in 1951. That year Williams was working as a core maker in a foundry, an episode that he would re-create vividly in the first chapter of his eighth novel, *The Junior Bachelor Society*. While on the job, he experienced a serious back injury that bothers him to this day. "I finally had to leave the foundry," remarked Williams, "because I couldn't do the work I did best and the other work simply didn't pay enough. I became a vegetable clerk at Loblaw's, a new supermarket. It was hiring some black help; nearly all of us were college graduates and a couple had advanced degrees."[13]

Unable to locate regular work in publishing or radio journalism, for which he had been trained, Williams applied in 1952 for a civil service job as a caseworker with the Onondaga County Welfare Department, where he remained until 1954, shifting after two years to children's worker. Williams recalls that there was "a lot of apprehensiveness about working with young mothers, mainly white. The job was both exhilarating and depressing—the first because if things were bad, you could always do something better with the kids, like take them away and place them in a decent home. And it was depressing because I realized that child abuse was an endless, horrible condition in the country and quite possibly the world."[14] In keeping with the autobiographical contours of his fiction, the protagonist in Williams's seventh novel, *Mothersill and the Foxes*, who is partially an avatar of the author, tries literally and symbolically to take care of the dispossessed children of the world, finally succeeding at the end of this provocative, zany, but ultimately flawed work. Williams's own enthusiasm for his job at welfare did not last. He landed a public relations job with Doug Johnson Associates, which he wove into his caseload, even as he continued as local correspondent for *Jet* and various periodicals.

Williams also had been writing poetry since 1946, publishing some of it in small magazines like *Poetry Book*, *Experiment*, and *Dilemma*. In 1953 he assembled twenty-three of his poems and, using his own money, produced a thin, gray volume that went on sale in Syracuse book stores that October. Written in free verse, without any rigorous attention to the relationship between syntax and poetic line, these poems—much like Faulkner's early work in *The Marble Faun*—are not highly distinguished. Unlike Faulkner's verse, however, with its Swinburnean derivations and sentiments, Williams seeks in *Poems* an authentic voice, one that would ultimately serve him well in his fiction. In his poetry of this very early period, Williams creates cultural images and artifacts in an idiom appropriate to the subjects. One of the best poems, "The Cool One," while lacking the clipped, syncopated rhythms of Gwendolyn Brooks's "We Real Cool," indicates Williams's skill in handling idiom and projecting imagery to make a cultural statement. This poem, written in 1950, begins:

> His back slouched, and excellently casual,
> The Cool One, finely draped, swings practiced
> Eyes disdainfully, walks apart from the
> epidemic crowds of summer New York.

What "The Cool One" and other poems in the collection reveal is an artist in his midtwenties trying to locate both a vision and a control over subject matter. Whether in a poem to his mother, "To Ola," several poems on music and dance, or in "Foundry," Williams was exploring subjects that he later would transmute successfully into his fiction over a twenty-five-year period.

Gradually Williams's growing intention to be a writer began to conflict with his need for a regular paycheck, as well as with the needs of his wife and two children. "I wasn't content to be able to wear a shirt, tie, and suit," Williams has confessed, "but my wife was."[15] During this period, Williams wanted to take a job with a black radio station in LeMoyne, Tennessee, but Carolyn did not want to relocate, preferring the security of her husband's welfare job, a conflict that Williams would review fictively in his first novel, *One for New York*. According to Williams, the string finally ran out in 1954. His brother Joe flew East, and

together they drove to Los Angeles, where Williams spent
the most miserable year of his life. Yet it was a year that pro-
pelled him toward his vocation as a writer.

One for New York

John Williams's mother, brother, and one sister had moved
to Los Angeles in 1948. (The other sister was living in Penn-
sylvania, married to a preacher who later became insane.)
But Williams could never take hold of California. He did
occasional publicity for NBC and CBS, worked for slick
real estate agents who exploited him, and ultimately was
employed by Golden State Mutual Life Insurance Company,
a black corporation rife with nepotism. It was a "family affair." The pay was low, but there was a sense of status, with
officers coming around each morning to shake Williams's
hand. Williams also remembers that the kitchen was excellent and that the meal ticket helped.

Perhaps because of creative block caused by distaste for
Los Angeles, which, he declares, "to this day I detest with
every bone in my body,"[16] Williams has never woven his
California experience into the autobiographical texture of
his novels in any significant manner. But there is one short
story, the widely anthologized "Son in the Afternoon," that
ranks with Faulkner's neglected "Golden Land" as one of
the best short fiction critiques of Los Angeles culture. Written in the mid-1950s but not published until 1962, "Son in
the Afternoon" is a concentrated, highly ritualistic, first-
person narrative of a black protagonist, Wendell, and the
retribution he seeks from an oppressive world. Employed as
a Hollywood scriptwriter, Wendell is one of the author's first
presentations of the successful middle-class professional—perhaps the dominant archetype in his fiction.
Wendell drives to Santa Monica to pick up his mother, who
is a maid for the affluent Couchman family. Forced to wait
there because Mrs. Couchman has not yet returned and ener-
vated by the unmannerly behavior of nine-year-old Ronnie
Couchman, Wendell contrives a minor victory over the
white race. When Kay Couchman enters the house in a
slightly intoxicated state and appears receptive to Wendell's

overtures, the protagonist (with the sharp eye of the good Grade B scriptwriter that he is) contrives to create a scene in which Ronnie sees his mother in the embrace of a black man. While this brief summary indicates the melodramatic quality of the tale, it does not account fully for its deeper resonances and subtleties. There are complex, quintessential renditions of mother-son and black-white relations, as well as shrewd presentation of the sexual and racial circuitry existing within the American experience. Williams controls perfectly the narrative angle in the story. Through his protagonist, the author persistently forces the reader to _perceive_ (a significant motif in the story is Wendell's litany, "you see") the Watts-Hollywood-Santa Monica topography that frames the action as a racial battleground. In "Son in the Afternoon" we have a small, charged arena in which Williams dramatizes the very themes that he would address more fully in his novels.

The story was written in New York. Williams had moved there in the summer of 1955. "I missed my kids," Williams has stated. "I had a very heavy guilt thing about them, too, and in California I couldn't do a damned thing about it. I was thinking of a change. I was involved with a couple women out there, but each felt my dream to be a real writer was so much horseshit. So my head was already thinking New York, New York, where I could be near my kids and be somewhere, perhaps, where the atmosphere was more conducive, gave more encouragement to write."[18] But employment was again a prerequisite for writing, and Williams took jobs, first as a staff member for special events programs at Columbia Broadcasting System, then in late 1955 as a publishing agent for a vanity press, Comet Books. Williams earned seventy-five dollars a week at Comet, and his room rent was thirty-six dollars. His experiences with Comet, a largely negative exposure to the exploitation of authors by editors and publishers, would serve as the basis of his first novel, _One for New York_, completed in 1956 but not published (under another title—_The Angry Ones_) until 1960. Before completing this novel, Williams had quit Comet and obtained a divorce. Subsequently he edited and published the _Negro Market Newsletter_ and served as an assistant to the publisher of Abelard-Schumann. In 1958 he traveled to

Europe as a correspondent for *Ebony* and *Jet*, the first of
several overseas trips that would shape Williams's evolving
vision and permit him to create unique international themes
in some of his best fiction.

Whether overseas or based in New York, Williams kept
writing fiction. In 1960 his first novel was published following at least three draft revisions, and in 1961 he published his
second New York novel, *Night Song*, patterned in part on
the legendary career of Charlie Parker. Unlike his first novel,
which had been largely ignored, *Night Song*, with its vivid
chronicling of the interracial jazz universe of Greenwich
Village, received some favorable reviews.[19] John Williams
was now 36 and living in Greenwich Village himself, and
starting on another novel, *Simon* (which would never be
completed). At this time, a member of the panel proposing
nominations for the Prix de Rome, sponsored jointly by the
American Academy in Rome and the American Academy of
Arts and Letters, was recommending the author as a prime
candidate for an award.

The Prix de Rome Affair

On January 23, 1962, the American Academy of Arts and
Letters notified John Williams's publishers, Farrar, Straus
and Cudahy, that their author had been selected for the Prix
de Rome, subject to his ability to accept the award. Williams
promptly accepted the fellowship, and the American
Academy of Arts and Letters was informed of his decision.
The President of the American Academy of Arts and Letters
wrote to Williams on January 30 that he had been selected
"subject to the approval of the American Academy in
Rome."[20] The president went on to discuss the stipend of
$3,500, transportation, incidentals, and residency at the
Academy in Rome. Events that followed constitute one of
the most bizarre, confusing, and disturbing episodes in contemporary American letters.

In mid-February of 1962 Williams had an interview with
Richard Kimball, a Yale-trained architect who was the Director for the American Academy in Rome. The interview,
which took place in Kimball's office at 101 Park Avenue,
was, Williams had heard, a mere formality—all past creative

writing fellows, including William Styron, Richard Wilbur, Ralph Ellison, and John Ciardi had been duly confirmed. Kimball declared that he had read part of *Night Song*, and went on to discuss living accommodations for the prize fellows in Rome, and the need for "fitting in." The interview, lasting about fifteen minutes, was cordial enough according to Williams. But on February 28, he received a letter from Felicia Geffen of the American Academy of Arts and Letters indicating that the American Academy in Rome had rejected the recommendation that he be elected to fellowship. Instead, Williams would be offered an award of $2,000. "There will be a luncheon before the ceremonial, which you and your fiance are cordially invited to attend."[21]

John Williams had been the unanimous first choice for the Prix de Rome by the American Academy of Arts and Letters jury, which that year was composed of John Hersey, Dudley Fitts, Louise Bogan, Phyllis McGinley, S. J. Perelman, Robert Coates, and John Cheever. The panel apparently never realized that its role was purely advisory, for all its previous decisions had been treated as definitive and final. Thus the panelists themselves were bewildered by the reversal of their decision and several, notably Hersey, were outraged. Writing to Williams from his residence in Weston, Connecticut, Hersey declared:

> Not having heard or read about this rukus, I was horrified to get your note. Hope to do something about those Rome people next week—small comfort to you at this point, I realize. That was a hell of a fine novel. The important thing is that you must write us more like that.

> With warmest regards,
> John Hersey

Essentially, however, nothing could be done to alter the decision that must have been taken by Kimball to deny Williams the Prix de Rome. There were vigorous protests from Williams's publisher, and requests by the author for clarification that went unheeded. Planning for the May 24 American Academy of Arts and Letters award ceremony continued without interruption, with the Academy printing up announcements of its program listing Alan Dugan as the recipient of the Prix de Rome and Williams as recipient of the se-

cond prize of $2,000. On May 7 Williams wrote to the AAAL:
"The events leading up to the granting of the award are of
such an ambiguous nature that I cannot in good conscience
accept the grant. . . . I feel now were I to accept the award,
it would be tacit agreement that no explanation was due
me."[22]

Quite clearly, it was Kimball who obstructed Williams's
nomination, but the former director over the years has refused to clarify the episode. Williams had arrived for his interview with Kimball wearing a tight cap and sporting a
pointed, "mephistophelian" beard, as the author calls the
goatee that he still has today. Williams was quiet, almost shy,
and restrained. But Kimball apparently was looking for more
special signs. Having perused *Night Song*, Kimball knew that
one character was on drugs, that another was an alcoholic,
that there were interracial relationships between men and
women in the novel. In retrospect, it seems fair to infer that
Kimball did not care for the subject matter of *Night Song*,
and that he believed Williams to be an extension of the
world he had written about in the novel, notably in relation
to the use of drugs. This was an erroneous assumption, for
those who have known John Williams acknowledge his long-
standing and abiding aversion to narcotics use. In any case,
Kimball concluded that a hastily conceived second candidate, poet Alan Dugan, elevated to runner up, would profit
more from a year in Rome.

Dugan shocked the guests invited to the American
Academy of Arts and Letters ceremony held in its auditorium
on May 24, 1962, by denouncing its connection with the
American Academy in Rome. "John Williams declined the
Arts and Letters Grant," stated Dugan, "because he was
refused the Academy in Rome Fellowship after having been
the unanimous choice of the jury of the National Institute of
Arts and Letters. This was done in an atmosphere of great
bureaucratic confusion. . . . My personal position is: I will
take the money from the Academies during their confusion—I can put it to good use—and I will go to Rome in
hopes that they behave better in their future awards." John
Williams also would salvage something from the affair,
transcribing the episode into *The Man Who Cried I Am*. On

September 24, 1962, the Board of Directors of the American Academy of Arts and Letters passed a resolution discontinuing the relationship between their body and the American Academy in Rome.

Middle Passage

Even as the American Academy of Arts and Letters was severing its ties with the American Academy in Rome, larger conflicts and confrontations were emerging in the United States that would have a greater impact on the scope and substance of John Williams's fiction than the scandal itself. James Meredith was enrolling at the University of Mississippi, testing 114 years of segregation at that institution and launching America into one of the more turbulent decades in its history. In keeping with the tenor of the times, Williams was also becoming more active in social and political movements. Since 1960 he had been a fund raiser and writer for the Committee for a Sane Nuclear Policy, an affiliation that would bring him to the attention of the FBI and the CIA, both of which have files on him.[23] To an extent, Williams's residence in New York City was also a catalyst for his changing perceptions. Trying to find apartments was horrendous because of the degree of discrimination. Beyond this stark reality, however, he was fitting into big city life. He basically enjoyed being in New York. He liked being able to go away on extended trips and to come back to *his* city.

Increasingly in the 1960s John Williams expanded and refined his vision of American culture to reflect the social and political dissonances of an evolving decade. By the time of the publication of his third novel, *Sissie*, in 1963, he was already examining people through history, dealing seriously for the first time in his career with generations in the life of a black American family, and creating a geography stretching fom Europe to New York to Syracuse to Los Angeles. *Sissie*, the story of the Joplin family, came out early in 1963 during the New York newspaper strike—not an encouraging coincidence for Williams in terms of prospective reviews and sales. Williams was pleased by the quality of *Sissie*, and to this day he "feels good" about it, as he indicated in an interview on February 24, 1981. He was working with new technical structures, creating points of departure in his handling of time. Moreover, in conceiving the Joplins, he was launching a family saga that he would retain a sense of touch with throughout his career, carrying certain family members with him right up to *!Click Song* (1982). With *Sissie*, John Williams had arrived as a mature and important writer of fiction.

The residual optimism implicit in the tone of *Sissie* lingered in Williams's work during 1963. Writing in the September 1963 issue of *Ebony*, the author declared bravely that "America resounds with the tread of Freedom Walkers and Riders. From the top of the country to the nitty-gritty bottom, change is in the air" (76). Yet Williams was a pragmatist, too, and when he embarked on a national trip for *Holiday* in September of 1963, a four-month journey through America, he knew pretty well what to expect. (He even tried to take rifles with him, but Ford Motor Company, which was sponsoring him with a bright white station wagon, refused to have its image tarnished by a gun-toting reporter.) Williams came away from his pilgrimage sobered by the racism that he had encountered in all parts of the country; heartened by the winds of change and the good people he had met; depressed by the quality of black education in the United States; and finally somewhat surprised by his residual commitment to the hope and promise of the American experiment. The provocative narrative emerging from his journey, *This Is My Country Too* (1965), is a minor classic in the literary history of a disquieting decade.

Producing virtually a book a year from 1960 to 1970, as well as dozens of articles, John Williams as artist and commentator traced the stages of stress and ultimately despair in a darkening decade. Not even his marriage to Lorrain Isaac in 1965, a personal affirmation of love in a disquieting world, and the birth of a son, Adam, in 1968, could alleviate the evolving spirit of pessimism in his oeuvre. During the decade he became preoccuped with conspiracies, assassinations, and genocide. Starting with his fourth and most celebrated novel, *The Man Who Cried I Am* (1967) and continuing through *Captain Blackman* (1972), John Williams created

political testaments to national failure. His extensive travels
across the United States, Europe, and Africa enabled him to
observe the United States from both within and without,
helping him (as it had Richard Wright) to confirm his perception of men and women functioning as political creatures in
a world geared to exploitation and oppression. Taking a
militant stand against all varieties of oppression, Williams
entered into the most activist period of his life, whether it involved participation in the march on Washington in 1963 or
help in the organization of the Black Academy of Arts and
Letters in 1968. At an organizational meeting of the Black
Academy on October 5, 1968, Williams stated: "I'm here
tonight because on the face of it the Black artists in this country have been completely neglected. . . . I remember Richard
Wright tried to get a $10,000 advance and it was denied
even after publishing 12 books. We need an Academy to
eliminate the inequalities that exist between black and white
artists." As one critic observed perceptively, Williams's
work in the 1960s was the "best barometer in American fiction of the mood of black America."²⁴ More significantly,
John Williams was measuring, better than any novelist of the
decade, the barometric pressure of an entire nation drifting
through successive social and political traumas.

The weight of history, starting with the cataclysmic events
of 1964—the killing of four girls in a Birmingham Baptist
church; the murders of the three civil rights workers in
Philadelphia, Mississippi; the riots in Harlem, Chicago, and
Philadelphia—clearly overwhelmed the author, deepening
his personal and literary vision. Whether writing a cynical
meditation on the life of Martin Luther King, Jr. (*The King
God Didn't Save*, 1970) or predicting a surprising end to
American military history (*Captain Blackman*, 1972),
Williams presents a panorama of exploitation by white
civilization of black culture. The imaginary King Alfred Plan
for black genocide that he devised in *The Man Who Cried I
Am* (a novel that Williams started in 1964 and spent three
and a half years writing) is a paradigm for the murderousness
perceived by the author to be at the heart of history. If conspiracies tend to circumscribe his work both in fiction and
nonfiction during the period, Williams assuredly did not

have very far to look. His harsh evaluation of King must be considered from this perspective, for Williams felt at the time and still does today that "ML" was a fool to have permitted himself to be destabalized by the FBI and the media. Everything for Williams seemed to point toward liquidation, assassination, and mayhem. The protagonist in Williams's apocalyptic novel *Sons of Darkness, Sons of Light* (1970) dwells persistently on the dream of black genocide inherent in white racism. In a conversation with a black militant, Gene Browning intimates that white America is simply waiting for a paper-thin excuse to do to blacks what Hitler did to the Jews. Caught up himself in the violence of the period, absorbed by the traps and snares of history, John Williams projects in the powerful fiction of the middle phase a harrowing account of the contemporary condition. In part, he was assuming the role of the iconoclast and demystifier, a function that he still enjoys today. ("I find it very exciting to raise specters, or ghosts, or ha'nts," he declared in the February interview.) Nevertheless, conspiracies were inherent in the times, and Williams became perhaps the most distinctive chronicler in fiction of those draconian forces at work in American history during the decade of the 1960s.

Following the publication of *Captain Blackman* in 1972, John Williams reached a watershed in his life and literary career. His work subsequently reveals the private truce—if not peace—that he has struck with the world. In part, he adjusted both his vision and his lifestyle to accommodate changing realities, especially the political retreat from activism and confrontation that had characterized the 1960s. This shift in attitude is reflected in Williams's next two novels, *Mothersill and the Foxes* (1975) and *The Junior Bachelor Society* (1976), in which characters seem more concerned with themselves (sometimes to the point of narcissism, as with Odell Mothersill) than with causes. But Williams was also receiving a measure of recognition and financial stability. Previously on the fringes of academic life, Williams in 1973 was awarded a Distinguished Professorship at the City University of New York. Creating new directions for himself, he thereby started a career as a full-time college teacher. After four years at the City University of New York, he moved to

Boston University in 1978, and the following year to Rutgers University at Newark, New Jersey, as a tenured professor. He now lives in Teaneck, New Jersey, close to campus life but still within striking distance of the city that continues to shape his fiction.

Recognition as an important literary artist has come slowly to John Williams, and the quest for success has tempered his work as a novelist. He actually was close to forty-five years of age before the literary in-group began to take him seriously. As an outspoken critic of the Establishment, and specifically its ghettoization of minority writers, he has been somewhat of an irascible figure, not making his passage through the publishing world any easier. In the February 22, 1981, issue of the *New York Times Book Review*, for example, he indicated that he felt that the rush to publish writing by black Americans had peaked quickly, and that many black writers were in the 1980s finding themselves back in an earlier era. Speaking of the difficulties he encountered in placing *!Click Song*, Williams observed: "A number of people looked at it and I was struck by their responses; they were much like those I used to get when I started writing in the 50s. It's almost as if we're going backward" (26). Significantly Williams's latest novel, which he spent seven years writing, is about the literary establishment and the problems of black and white writers. Fiction once again for Williams reflects in its theme the author's own tenacious and principled quest to be an artist on his own terms. *!Click Song* adds to his stature as one of the most unique, prolific, and consequential American writers today. It also suggests yet another watershed as he moves beyond his earlier fiction. John Williams in the 1980s has emerged finally as a powerful force in the literary life of the Republic.

Chapter Two
Searching for America: The Nonfiction

Throughout his career, John Williams has used the craft of nonfiction to test many of the subjects and themes and to polish many of the stylistic techniques employed in his fiction. In fact, he published nonfiction before fiction in the 1950s, largely to make ends meet, undertaking assignments wherever he could get them. He has not ceased writing articles, although he admits in his introduction to *Flashbacks: A Twenty-year Diary of Article Writing* that "writing articles is no sane way for a man to make his living."[1] It was, however, Williams's literary and philosophical apprenticeship, a vehicle used by the author to investigate the contours of culture and to make a significant statement about social problems. "The article gets to the point as no other genre,"[2] Williams once observed. As essayist and nonfiction book writer, Williams is very much in a tradition extending from W. E. B. DuBois to contemporaries like James Baldwin, artists who use nonfiction prose as a weapon to attack, as Williams himself has declared, "the cruelty and stupidity of the white American society."[3]

While Williams is capable of excoriating the white world, he is far more interested in both his nonfiction and fiction in the totality of American civilization—in the confluence of race, class, caste, and sex in the dynamics of a nation's history. Scarcely satisfied with lodging a litany of crimes by whites against blacks, he focuses more typically in his nonfiction on a nation at war with itself. People on both sides of the color line are frequently obtuse and blind to the facts of history as well as to contemporary realities. Intensely personal at times, but also by turns philosophical, clinically observant, or analytical, Williams in his nonfiction probes the crucial question of whether men and women can transcend the limitations and traps often set for them by history.

Thus the prime concern of his nonfiction dovetails with that of the fiction. Speaking of his articles, Williams acknowledged in an interview: "Researching and writing them gave me ideas and material which in some form or other went into my novels."[4] Whether helping to ghostwrite a book on narcotics enforcement early in his career or writing about minorities in the city at a later stage,[5] Williams through his nonfiction has learned about the workings of America, and this has deepened his vision of the national panorama that unfolds in his fiction. The autobiographical elements, the naturalistic emphases, the documentary mode, the political reflections: these elements characteristic of Williams's nonfiction are also the hallmarks of his novels. His attention especially to the craft of the article—the demands of space, the need for precise focus, the attention to detail and fact— all served the author in controlling the increasingly complex canvasses that he created in his fiction. Today Williams still prefers to have a nonfiction work in progress alongside projects in fiction. Mirrored persistently in the nonfiction of John Williams are the vision and craft of the novelist.

The Artist in America

Few authors have written more eloquently about the trials and passages of black artists—and by extension, black professionals—in America than John Williams. Acknowledging "a difference in approach to 'consciousness' between black and white writers,"[6] Williams combats nevertheless the tendency to ghettoize black artists that occurs at the primary level by treating them as a unique species divorced from the broader American culture domain. This also involves subtle institutional mechanisms that reflect poorly on the artistic establishment in America. Williams has traced the pattern of the ghettoization of black artists in America, moving from the period in literary history when there was only enough space for one Richard Wright or James Baldwin to the flush years in the 1970s when all "Negro stuff," as Williams once overheard a literary agent refer to it, was a hot commodity, to the more recent benign neglect of work by black writers. Compounding the problem is the fact, which Williams has addressed, that most black Americans do not read serious literature by black or white artists. For whom, then, do black American artists create? Who, if any, are their mentors? Can they escape ghettoization in order to see, in Williams's words, how their work might stack up against that by figures such as William Styron?

Williams addressed these issues early in his career. In a 1963 essay entitled "The Literary Ghetto," he speaks of the "labeling" that affects black writers. "Almost without fail, a novel written by a Negro is said to be one of anger, hatred, rage, or protest. Sometimes modifiers are used: 'beautiful' anger, 'black' hatred, 'painful' rage, 'exquisite' protest. These little tickets deprive the novel of any ability it may have to voice its concern for all humankind, not only Negroes."[7] Concomitant with the sins of labeling, declares Williams, is another crime, that of "grouping," in which critics treat a herd of black writers in one review, blurring distinctions and often forgetting the validity of individual texts. Both labeling and grouping are part of the larger trend of ghettoizing by comparing black writers only to members of their group.

Of course, within the classification schemes for black ghettoization, there are subtle variations. One, which Williams analyzes with reference to his second novel, *Night Song*, is the obtuseness if not outright hostility of white reviewers to the presentation of mixed couples by black writers. Williams asserts that there is a double standard here: "The relationship between mixed couples is always more graciously accepted by the reviewers when related by a white author than by a Negro. Jack Kerouac's one-dimensional Negro girl and her white lover, John Updike's quiet, fleeting references to the same combination, and Robert Gover's hilarious team of Kitten and James Cartwright Holland are a few examples."[8] Confined to a literary ghetto, despite the illusion that they have actually emerged from it because of increased interest by publishers, talented black writers in the 1960s were encountering obstacles to the expansion and diversification of their productions.

In another essay written in 1963, "The Negro in Literature Today," Williams examined a paradox inherent in the proliferation of black literary talent. "If the Negro has nothing else," he wrote, "he has had the truth of American hypocrisy in the marrow of his bones. A Negro writer does not escape the fate of the average Negro. He has shared it to the full and has come to know the hollowness at the core, with each achievement, of the society he is applauded by."[9] Bound to the larger dimension of racial conflict in America, the black artist develops, according to Williams, a fundamental antipathy toward white writers and white critics—indeed, the entire literary establishment. Ten years later in an interview, Williams would reassert this animus, noting of this attitude that "it's an antipathy that is well deserved, because certainly the white literary establishment understands very well what it's about. It propagates white values and standards, and black writers, in order to be credited and accepted, would have to displace them entirely."[10] Williams knows how virulent the literary establishment can be and how easy it is for even the handful of black publishers and editors to be co-opted by it. Black publishers are not necessarily more sensitive than others to the struggles of unknown black writers seeking an audience, and they engage in the same contract malpractices that typify the larger world of publishing. Even more unfortunate, Williams indicates, is the failure of established black writers to lend support to the younger generation of talent. He is somewhat reserved and oblique in his criticism, but it is evident that he feels that the counterparts of earlier literary mentors like Langston Hughes, Richard Wright, and Chester Himes do not exist on the contemporary scene, although there are several artists of sufficient stature to serve this important nurturing function. Gently chastising certain figures for their self-conscious condemnation of lesser black talent, Williams points out that the essential problem is not one of talent but rather of the rigid conventions of the publishing world that determine who is "in" at any given time. In perhaps his most pointed statement of the dilemma, he has written, "We need Ellison and Baldwin to give a hand."[11]

Williams recognizes that with or without a support network, black artists in America must make their way in a marketplace geared to middle-class taste. Where does this coinci-

dence of economics, taste, and literary convention leave
black artists? Often, asserts Williams, these writers are disen-
franchised even on their own ground. Thus it is not surprising to Williams that William Styron should win critical praise
for his depiction of black history and experience in *The Confessions of Nat Turner*, while a fine, earlier novel about slave
rebellions, Arna Bontemps's *Black Thunder* (1936), should
remain unacclaimed. He observes laconically in his critique
of Styron's novel that white writers have taken over the
function of delineating the lives of black Americans: "Indeed, works by white writers on black people are considered to be more palatable and acceptable to the nation at
large than similar works by black writers. I hold John Clellan
Holmes's *The Horn* far and away the best work by a white
author on Negroes in contemporary times. I wish I had written it. I cannot say that Styron's book was honest; I have
doubts that even in intent it was honest."[12]

What Williams objects to in *The Confessions of Nat
Turner* is Styron's willful distortion of history. Labeling
Styron "a propagandist for white history," Williams declares that any author dealing with history must be of
necessity both a writer and a historian in the mode of Robert
Graves, Mary Renault, and Arna Bontemps. Treating Turner's
revolt as a unique act, Styron ignores the dozens of similar
insurrections documented by Woodson, Aptheker, and
others. Moreover, Styron lapses unconsciously into the role
of an apologist for the South, implying that free blacks suffered more than slaves. In the battle for historical accuracy
in the novelistic presentation of the truth of the black American experience, an individual like Styron, coddled by the
literary marketplace, prevails over other artists, black and
white, who strive for more authentic renderings of black
history.

With the growing success of Williams's own fiction in the
1960s and 1970s, one might expect a more temperate tone
to emerge with respect to the author's vision of the artist in
America. Yet the relevance of certain forces that constrict
the creativity and threaten the very survival of black artists
remains acute. Surveying the literary scene for the *Black
Scholar* in 1975, Williams addressed himself to the continu-

ing crisis in American letters. He ascribes this crisis to the fact that most white writers in the United States "can no longer speak generally or truthfully for all Americans," even as non-white writers continue to have difficulty publishing their versions of reality in America. Williams's accusations are based on persistent economic pressures and sociohistorical realities that perpetuate the crisis, despite waves of popularity that certain groups of writers might enjoy from time to time. The crisis is inherent in civilization itself, a civilization Williams maintains has "looped the world from east to west"[13] like a lethal rainbow.

In "The Crisis in American Letters" he analyzes the process of conflict in American letters as a reflection of the historical crisis in American race relations. Even as the contemporary world has changed radically, both America and American letters have lived by outdated suprematist codes designed to limit the amount of change in society. Moreover, to the extent that in the important work of American writers like Hemingway, Pound, Dreiser, Wolfe, and Faulkner there is an element of bigotry, Williams indicates truthfully the extent of readjustment required by American letters to purge itself of residual racism. "We have been treated to Faulkner's endurables, Mailer's black sex machines, Malamud's ex-con with a literary bent, Updike's jive militant on dope, and so on. This cannot be the essence of black or any other life."[14] As an antidote to white literary misrepresentations of the black experience, Williams asserts that black writers must speak out of and about the "politics of race," and that they must be granted access to those media outlets that can market their work.

Williams's portrait of the crisis in American letters is, of course, rendered from the point of view of an individual who experienced it, not only in the Prix de Rome episode, but at every stage in his progress as an artist. Despite the value judgments that he brings to the issue, there is both political wisdom and moral toughness in his constant affirmations of the need to fight for the survival of creativity in American society. The essential paradox for Williams is that to the extent that artists care to criticize society, they expose themselves to the danger that their own creativity might not survive. This cautionary insight is attended by the greater conviction that the task of the writer is to advise, enlarge, caution, and assuredly criticize. "The writer's role," asserts Williams, "is usually the adversary, the outsider, the Rover in the croquet game."[15] He is careful not to let readers forget the tradition of Thoreau, Douglass, Toomer, Wright, and others, a tradition based on the opposition of the American writer to perceived defects in the culture. We have always had our Solzhenitzyns, declares Williams. "Nearly all fledgling writers move in his direction. Their topics are in the main directed at injustice, at society's failures, compromises, untruths, which indicates to me that deep within the enchanted forest, fires are still burning, and that in the smithy of our souls spirits are at work welding a human consciousness."[16] For artists to align themselves with this tradition takes some courage, but it is a fundamental commitment that recurs in Williams's own fiction and in much of his nonfiction.

He seems to gravitate naturally and sympathetically toward black artists and celebrities who fit the tradition of protest. His essays and books on such figures as Richard Wright, Charlie Parker, Dick Gregory, Malcolm X, Marcus Garvey, Chester Himes, Romare Bearden, and Jack Johnson reveal effectively how the adversary role culminates in a tradition of opposition to the equalities and inequities in Western and specifically American civilization. His biography of Richard Wright, *The Most Native of Sons* (1970), written for young people, reflects Williams's belief in the moral necessity of the artist to make a didactically explicit statement about the politics of oppression. Richard Wright is a seminal figure, an artist in opposition who influenced Williams, notably in the texture of family life represented in *Sissie*, and whom the author presents in the character of Harry Ames ("the father of all contemporary writers" as one character terms him) in *The Man Who Cried I Am*.

The biography on Wright elaborates through a basic pattern of thematic repetition and variation the trials of the black artist in a hostile and virulently racist world. Drawing much of his material from Wright's books, Williams's study for a youthful audience stresses from the outset the seriousness of the subject matter: "Think of Mississippi and you think of white cotton and black people; you think of bigots who murder, and the years heavy with black blood. Of all the states in the American Union it has been the one most repressive for Negroes."[17] There is no need to trace this consistent tonality in the biography. What is significant is that Williams gives coherent and exact expression to the causal patterns underlying Wright's passage from the deep South to the North and ultimately into exile. Wright's life, as subsequent biographers like Addison Gayle have demonstrated, reads like an actual bildungsroman, not so much an artfully contrived fictive odyssey as a harrowingly real passage in which the protagonist confronts the fluid but deadly structure of Western civilization. Instructed to fear the power of the written word even as a youth, beguiled by a black editor who refused to pay him in 1924 for his first story (which he wrote in the eighth grade), forced to rebel against a graduation speech that had been written for him, Wright as a youth learned that language was a weapon, that it could be a tool of oppression or liberation. This is a central homily that Williams presents for his audience. He traces this particular literary code throughout Wright's career, demonstrating the ways in which Wright used his creative powers as an instrument of class struggle.

It is still a matter of conjecture whether the American government intelligence community had a role in Richard Wright's decline from literary fame to relative obscurity in the 1950s, or even if American agents assumed complicity in his death on November 28, 1960 (a connection implied by Williams in _The Man Who Cried I Am_ but not in the biography). At the very least we must assume, as Williams does, that powerful forces—not the least of them the publishing houses—caused the diminishment of a great artist and critical neglect of his later work that persists today. While Williams is interested in the life and death of Richard Wright as a man, he is also preoccupied with the evolution and passage of a great creative force. "What Richard did," writes Williams in his conclusion, "was to set forth the premise that America's basic ills were those of racism, which cut across questions of economics, political philosophies, religion, and national survival. He applied his premise to white western Christian civilization, and then widened his theory to include the racial situations existing between whites in Europe and blacks and browns in Asia and Africa'' (133–34). Williams himself learned much from the example of Wright, and his own movement outward from his origins to the international arena of conflict duplicates to an extent the pattern that he investigates in Wright's life and work.

There is an intricate unity, a sort of common pathology, involving the creative mind and his or her cultural conflicts that underlies Williams's assessments of black artists. Notably, in the series of articles collected in the Personalities section of *Flashbacks*, there is a fine symmetry involved in the presentation of creative artists caught in an insidious cultural context. All these essays, in fact, assert a conscious artifice and manipulation in white society's treatment of black artists. At best, as in the case of the artist and sculptor Romare Bearden, a period of benign neglect yields to begrudging recognition of genius. At worst, in the case of Charlie Parker, the progress of the black artist involves the saga of a genius overwhelmed by irreversible cultural calamities. Parker's life, declares Williams, "does not reflect the explosion of school desegregation or sit-in violence; it is the other, less picturesque extreme: the slow erosion of an exceptional Negro symbolic of the assonances and dissonances that are America" (*Flashbacks*, 222). In his article on Parker, written for *Swank* in 1960 and one of his best essays (the distillation of materials on Bird that he had hoped to make into a nonfiction book but which he finally transmuted into parts of *Night Song* and *Sissie*), Williams worked out the guiding principles for a type of prose, whether fiction or nonfiction, that focuses on the protagonist as a man of talent who is beset constantly by a hostile culture. Rejected by both white and black audiences, outraged by the contradictions in American culture, seeking solace in the nihilism of his favorite film, *The Wild One*, Parker burned himself out in his epic resistance to the banalities of American life: "Bird died amid a paroxym of laughter; he was watching the Kate Smith show with the Dorsey brothers. Jimmy had just been announced as the greatest saxophone player in the world" (*Flashbacks*, 231). The juxtaposition of these two representatives of jazz talent, of success and failure, of white and black, speaks to the essential condition of the black artist on the American scene that Williams explores in his work.

What Williams sees in the eyes of one of his favorite writers and literary friends, Chester Himes, "the pain of life as a black man and artist" (*Flashbacks*, 294), provides a unifying element of truth in his approaches to the reality of the black artist in American society. By concentrating on the assonances and dissonances in the lives of black artists, Williams exposes the gap between talent and recognition, the work and its reception. Himes, whom the author considers the greatest contemporary American naturalist, is still a largely neglected figure. It is true that *Cotton Comes to Harlem* was a commercial success, but Himes's total achievement remains unknown to both film and literary critics.

Neither the neglect nor the occasional adulation of critics alters the essential goal of black artists. " 'I work out of a response and need to redefine the image of man in terms of the Negro experience I know best,' " asserts Romare Bearden in the introduction that Williams wrote to his work (*Flashbacks*, 283). This statement is a powerful programmatic idea. Williams himself develops the concept in his appreciative essay on Bearden. "Black truth," he writes, "*projects* upon white consciousness another, more truthful image of man" (*Flashbacks*, 284). Black artistic truth reveals essentially a failure in the underlying structures of white Western civilization, and a proposal to set right those destructive social and political forces in culture. Williams elaborates this program in his linkage of the "distortions" in Bearden's work to the assonances and dissonances in the music of Charlie Parker, Miles Davis, Thelonius Monk, John Coltrane, and others who composed "'in color,' projected upon what was ordinary, acceptable, usual, mundane—white—a different sound, a changed pattern that was augmented, diminished and shaped by the personal and group experiences of the black men involved. They seemed to distort sound in order to recreate it" (*Flashbacks*, 288). To an extent this method is propagandistic, but Williams also asserts that it is finally redemptive. To redefine and enhance the image of humanity through the black experience becomes an unusual moral struggle, a grim but graceful effort to illuminate reality in order to comprehend it fully.

The Manipulation of History and Fact

For John Williams, any full comprehension of reality requires attention to the facts, and consequently a willingness by the artist to research, revise, and reconstruct history. The commitment to historical analysis is significant in both Williams's fiction and nonfiction, with the author persistently calling upon history in order that he might understand individual and collective destiny. Part of his goal in novels like *Captain Blackman* and books like *Africa: Her History, Lands and People* involves an attempt literally to retrieve history that has been abandoned or ignored by conventional writers and putative experts. But the author's largest objective in his work is to create an accurate *sense* of history as the key to recognizing the origins and contours of the contemporary condition.

Africa—and by extension the Afro-American experience—is the major element for Williams in the authentic re-creation and reinterpretation of history as it bears upon American civilization. Here, the need to re-create a usable past, using new historical evidence while at the same time demolishing old stereotypes and myths of the African past, is obvious to anyone familiar with twentieth-century scholarship. When Countee Cullen asked in his poem, "Heritage," "What is Africa to me?" he posed the fundamental dialectical question for black Americans, one reflected variously in other poems of the period such as McKay's "Outcast" and Hughes's "The Negro Speaks of Rivers." If America is an alien land for blacks and Africa, truly forgotten, a vast terra incognita of the cultural and historical imagination, then a special task for black artists is to trace that pattern of causality, a process carrying deep into the collective life of an entire culture, which might explain contemporary Afro-American realities. Seeking these mediating links between two cultures and two continents, Williams has visited Africa, incorporated Africa into his fiction, and worked sporadically on an "Africa" novel (as he calls it) that awaits future completion. What presently exists as his most vivid example of interest in the African past is a richly illustrated book, *Africa: Her History, Lands and People* (1962), another of his texts for young people.

A small, dedicated press, Cooper Square Publishers, brought out the book. By and large, during the period, the publishing world was not interested in providing black children—or white children for that matter—with the correct texts or critical tools needed to understand the contemporary world. In fact, the main reason that Williams has not written anything for young people since his 1970 biography of Richard Wright is the resistance he encountered to other proposals he had for children's books whose subjects disturbed the publishing community. "I discovered through my friends who write children's books," observed Williams on February 24, 1981, "that there you've got a formula. I wanted to do a book about children of interracial marriages. . . .When it came down to it, no one really wanted to get into that kind of stuff." Williams's own interracial marriage and the astute presentation of the subject in his fiction for adults would have made him the ideal writer of such a book. While admitting that he is now "too jaundiced" to return today to writing for young people, Williams retains a fondness for his Africa study, which has gone through three revisions and reprintings.

In *Africa: Her History, Lands and People*, Williams offers an evocative primer on this continent, positing as a controlling thesis the idea that to know the past is to engage in an act of conservation. As the great English historian J. H. Plumb has observed, "The past is always a created ideology with a purpose, designed to control individuals, or motivate societies, or inspire classes." For a young American audience, Williams must literally re-create the African past in order to establish a broad ideology testifying to the cultural significance of an entire continent and to its contemporary relevance. "Africa," he writes in his introduction, "is the past and the future; the cradle of life and its graveyard."[18] Writing the book at a time when more than twenty former colonies were coming to independence, Williams saw Africa as a subject for the presentation not only of "lost" history but for the examination of ambivalent historical forces that have shaped the modern Western political imagination.

Williams dispels the myth of Africa as terra incognita, a miasmic territory separated from other more advanced civilizations by raging rivers filled with fierce, howling monsters—the "raging river" syndrome that afflicted Thales, early European explorers, and even modern historians. As a related element in this effort to demystify Africa and its history, Williams presents a chronological and descriptive account of the continent, ranging from Zinjanthropus to the creation of Equatorial Guinea in 1968, stressing the indigenous contours of African civilization and the cross-cultural effects arising from the intersection of European, Middle Eastern, American, Oriental, and African civilizations. He attacks the myths of an Africa devoid of accomplishments, or whose key advances were created by people outside Africa. Although he does not engage in conceptual subtleties that would perplex his intended audience, he does stress implicitly the historical accomplishments of various African civilizations—Egyptian, Ethiopian, Carthaginian, Mali, Songhai, and others—while looking critically at the growing intrusion of European culture into the web of African history.

The chapter on slavery, "A Continent in Chains," while retaining a commitment to historical objectivity, comes closest to projecting that tone of critical political assessment that typifies Williams's best work in fiction and nonfiction. He writes: "As bad as slavery had been in the Orient, in Africa, in Europe—anywhere in the world—nothing like it existed until Europeans began plundering African coasts for human beings who had become more valuable than the gold they possessed" (23). Swiftly tracing the history of slavery, Williams emphasizes the special brutality of the African slave trade. The next chapter, "The Slaves Strike Back," offers a brief revisionist interpretation of slave rebellions in the New World. He selectively cites several of the more than 250 revolts to emphasize the tenacity of opposition by slaves to the dominant white civilization intent on keeping an entire race oppressed.

Williams's tone is less severe in those chapters devoted to white colonial intrusions into Africa during the great age of modern exploration. Such individuals as Mungo Parks, Richard Burton, and Livingstone and Stanley seem to fascinate Williams as much as they would a young audience. To an extent, this interest prevents him from examining with sufficient clarity the myths fostered by European travelers and commentators in the nineteenth and twentieth centuries. Even the best of these explorer-writers, Burton, could not transcend stock stereotyping or homilies on the need to improve the African morally, just as explorers after him would attempt to foster the idea that Africa was in need of Victorian uplift. Williams, of course, does not succumb to the romance of the age of exploration; and in chapters on the Zulu and on the great powers' grab for Africa in the modern age, he retains a critical objectivity. "Even as Stanley, Livingstone, and the parade of explorers snaked through Africa's jungles," he writes, "African warriors girded to fight the white trespassers" (48). The Boers, England, France, Germany, Portugal, Spain: one European country after another maneuvered to obtain sovereignty over parts of the African continent, bringing with them an ideological grammar that submerged the African identity.

Williams has difficulty sustaining this philosophical-historical edge in the last section of the book, which is essentially a potpourri of African geography, tribal customs, and indigenous art, capped by a factfinder on new African states. Given the encyclopedic nature of the challenge that any short book on Africa must contend with, Williams succeeds in introducing his subject and in providing a panorama of Africa for the young audience. He presents the myths and realities of the continent in a graphic and accessible way. History, Williams seems to contend, involves a persistent search for a usable past. In this quest, no people or cultural group can afford to neglect its origins.

History and its Heroes: Martin Luther King, Jr.

If ignorance of history is one form of cultural genocide, then distortion of it is equally insidious. This assertion, as indicated earlier, forms the cutting edge of Williams's critique of *The Confessions of Nat Turner*. He offers a much more comprehensive indictment of historical distortion in his assessment of Martin Luther King, Jr., in *The King God Didn't Save* (1970). Williams subtitles this controversial study "Reflections on the Life and Death of Martin Luther King, Jr.," and in essence it can be read best as a philosophical inquiry into the making of American heroes rather than as any detailed or definitive account of King's life. In fact, Williams asserts today that the book is much more a "meditation" than pure biography. Although the civil rights movement serves as the historical bedrock of the book, Williams is concerned primarily with why Martin Luther King became such a charismatic figure, a celebrity of contemporary American history. His thesis—that King served the needs of the American power structure even more than he symbolized the aspirations of black Americans—is revisionist in its refusal to celebrate a contemporary hero, and radical in its systematic attempt to demystify an individual trapped ultimately by historical forces that he could not manage or control.

In his dedication to "the memory of the man Martin Luther King could have become, had he lived," Williams reveals the uncompromisingly critical tone he strikes in the study. He follows this initial signal with an epigram taken from Richard Wright's *Black Power* that reveals the philosophy of history that he plans to apply:

Make no mistake . . . they are going to come at you with words about democracy; you are going to be pinned to the wall and warned about decency; plump-faced men will mumble academic phrases . . . . gentlemen of the cloth will speak unctuously of values and standards; in short, a barrage of concentrated arguments will be hurled at you to temper the pace and drive of your movement . . . .

Even if we were to dismiss any hidden reference to King in Williams's decision to reproduce these lines at the outset, it would be impossible to overlook the lesson that both he and Wright want us to derive from the study of historical movements. The values and goals of movements can be co-opted by more powerful outside groups representing a fundamentally conservative political system. Writing his study of King in the late 1960s, Williams projects the same pessimistic pattern of thought characteristic of his major novels of the period, *The Man Who Cried I Am*, *Sons of Darkness, Sons of Light*, and *Captain Blackman*. He is sympathetic to the role of the artist as rebel in his biography of Wright. Conversely, he is critical of the life of Martin Luther King, Jr., whom he proceeds to treat as a figure defeated by history and events. "This is a study of Martin Luther King, Jr.," he writes, "a unique man in many ways, but it is also a study of the awesome exercise of power in the United States, and it was this power, finally, that cut King down in conspiracy, and then conspired to plug the memory of this man with putty."[19]

History for Williams is "philosophy teaching by examples," to invoke Bolingbroke's phrase. The key example is, of course, King, who is presented as a man shaped by events and made to do service in the cause of the Establishment. "As a spider spins out its web," observes Williams at the start of his inquiry, "so America had spun out the brutal destiny of Martin King" (19). Alternately subjective, meditative, and critically detached, making it known to the reader that he, too, was involved in the movement, Williams sets out to explore the philosophical tensions between violent and nonviolent protest that he sees at the base not only of King's life and the cause he came to represent, but at the root of American history itself.

Williams divides the work into two roughly equal parts, "The Public Man" and "The Private Man"—an antiphonal chorus in which King's public posturing serves as an index of his personal strengths and weaknesses. Part 1, consisting of eleven chapters, traces King's career from 1954 to his assassination on April 4, 1968. Part 2, nine chapters, places events against the backdrop of King's personal life, dealing with notable ethical, religious, and class components that molded him. Many chapters in the first part focus on specific years of the civil rights movement, and thus serve as a chronicle of key historical events. Unifying both sections is Williams's own perception of what he terms at a later stage "the manipulation of white power" (173), which managed to contain King and therefore his movement. If, as Williams acknowledges, Martin Luther King "really, really got under my skin" (119), it was not simply because Gregory, the author's oldest son, wanted to become a minister. More to the point, it was because of King's failure to perceive fully or in time the nakedness of white power in its dealings with black Americans: "King, believing he had power, attacked the white power structure. He did not understand that it had armed him with feather dusters" (172). Examining this book and Williams's fiction of the period, we see clearly the author's preoccupation with power as a shaping force—indeed the sole determinant—in history.

According to Williams, King fit the mold of the traditional figure of the black minister, "one white people are used to and find extremely comforting" (29). The public, politicians, the press—even white segregationists—created King. He was the apostle of nonviolence, a reassuring figure when juxtaposed against the militants of Black Power and the turbulence of the times. Thus King fit into the tradition of orderly democratic process. Williams's task as historian, philosopher, and biographer is to demystify the man and to offer an interpretation of him that is more critical than that of other studies, that deals aggressively with the failure of the individual and the co-optation of his movement.

Williams offers numerous incidents detailing King's failures as a public figure and his submission to white power. For example, the 1960 Atlanta sit-ins at Rich's and Davidson's department stores, mediated by King, resulted in the stores opening again on the same segregated basis. King's subsequent arrest and incarceration along with other young Southern Christian Leadership Conference (SCLC) protestors was turned to beneficial political purposes, in an election year, by the Kennedys, who intervened directly and powerfully to gain King's release: "King's thunder had been lifted, and neatly. He had been used to secure the votes of the masses, and it was not important whether he liked the Kennedys or not" (47).

Preoccupied with philosophical implications of political activity, Williams explores a paradox: Martin Luther King was perhaps the most famous black man in the world, the winner of the Nobel Prize for peace, yet he was a failure.

Possessing fundamental reservations about the philosophy of nonviolence, Williams offers a deterministic view of King as a man shaped by public history. In fact, although the second part of the study is captioned "The Private Man," Williams is far more interested in explaining King through the basic cultural patterns of color, education, vocation, and class than in offering details about his personal life. The last three chapters, which are devoted to the scandal over King's sex life that was generated by J. Edgar Hoover, are an unfortunate departure—"pious porno" as one reviewer termed it[20]—from the philosophical inquiry; they are relevant only to the extent that they reinforce Williams's investigation of the conspiracy of power that molded and ultimately destroyed King.

Martin Luther King, Jr., engages Williams's sympathy only to the extent that he *could* have become great. Williams almost wishes greatness for his subject, and this yearning accounts for the complex, confusing, even contradictory tones in the study that range from anger to lamentation. The author did have difficulties coming to terms with his subject. Both the stylistic excesses and factual inaccuracies stem from his ambivalent attitude toward King, as well as his intimate involvement in the movement King led. Writing about the original Freedom Ride in May 1961, Williams cannot locate adequate language or calibrate style to render the horrors awaiting the twelve participants who journeyed South in Trailways and Greyhound buses: "The crackers came in the grip of their white sickness, as eager to hurt and maim those who had chosen to be defenseless, as the syphilis-ridden sailors of Elizabethan England had been to go to Africa to enslave—after they had raped every black girl and woman they could put their pox-polluted phalluses to" (49). Here, blatant editorializing and melodramatic excess tend to diminish the event and the author's insight. Williams is far more effective when his style is more modulated, more matched to the historical, as in this section from his account of the Birmingham protests in the spring of 1963:

Most of all we recall the well-fed police dogs caught in mid-air by the camera's lens, caught inches away from the bodies of black teenagers, as policemen wearing sunglasses stood wide-legged at the end of the leashes. And who has forgotten the black youngsters, as if in a rain dance, being swept back, their arms outstretched, their legs braced against the wet grasses at Kelly Ingram Park, and the firemen whose high-pressure hoses were trained on them? (56)

The balanced cadences, the cinematic sweep, and the image of the children indicate stylistic brilliance found intermittently throughout the study.

Ultimately, the strength of this work hinges not so much on matters of style as on the validity of his interpretation. Williams implies that there is nothing simple or straightforward about King's life or about the historical forces that converged on the man. Reluctantly embracing the Vietnam protest movement toward the end of his life, King saw his own popularity affected, in part because he was breaking the mold created for him and operating in new paths of power. Beset by the FBI, he made concessions and accommodations, while the press, assuming complicity in his eclipse, devoted less attention to the goals of his nonviolent movement. Alluding to King in an interview, Williams indicates that "given the times in which we live, one ought to be more knowledgeable about where movements are going." Williams does not gloss over the failure of Martin Luther King to ward off the assaults through him on the movement. Assassination, never merciful, did come when King was in decline.

Charles A. Beard once observed that it is always dangerous to reduce human affairs to some law of "total historical unfolding." To an extent, Martin Luther King, Jr., as projected by Williams, is a formula figure in whom we witness the history of the times. Ultimately, the "facts" of history are at the mercy of subjective interpretation, and Williams, writing in the whirlwind of an era given to pessimism and protest, renders a singular portrait. It is a unique explanation or meditation upon personality and historical process, and one that must be read carefully and critically as contemporary record. Nevertheless, within the context of Williams's oeuvre, *The King God Didn't Save* is a sharp, provocative account of the author's vision of America.

Searching for America

The inability of John Williams to come to terms with Martin Luther King in the late 1960s was in part a reflection of the larger difficulties he encountered throughout the entire decade in coming to terms with America. Throughout the 1960s, he was searching for America, trying to locate some sustaining national vision that might be relevant to him. The origins of this quest are recorded in one of his most poignant works, *This Is My Country Too* (1965), the record of a trip he took in 1963 across the United States in search of that elusive American spirit that has captivated and spurred American writers from the earliest explorers, through Thoreau, to such contemporary apostles of the road as Henry Miller, Jack Kerouac, and John Steinbeck. Alluding to his odyssey in *The King God Didn't Save*, he writes, "I took to the road on a long trip to see what the nation was like, thinking *that* was a time of racial crisis!" (65).

This Is My Country Too, developed originally on commission as a two-part article for *Holiday* and published subsequently in expanded form as a book, is Williams's response to this tradition of white writers commenting on their journeys in America. It is a pointed rejoinder to Steinbeck's commercially popular *Travels with Charley* (1962). "I was to travel with Mr. Charlie," Williams observed (*Flashbacks*, 34). Offered in a different key, Williams's account is a harrowing but at the same time wonderfully modulated narrative of a unique journey. In its own way, the book reaffirms the unending quest for harmony in America, and it is this vision that we detect as the latent strength and center of gravity, one that occasionally is suppressed by the author but which always reasserts itself in John Williams's work.

Williams acknowledges the strength of the American dream at the outset of *This Is My Country Too*, even as he, like Steinbeck, detects moral ambiguities in the American grain. "Late in September 1963," he begins, "I set out in search of an old dream, one that faded, came back into focus, and faded again. The search was for my America."[21] This search begins appropriately with the author's return to the city where he grew up and where he first learned about

America. "I drove north, of course, and west, for a search begins at a point where the hunter was believed lost. For me, it was Syracuse" (7). Williams offers a vivid remembrance of his childhood in Syracuse during the Depression, recalling memories of the Goodyear blimp, Glenn Miller's music, and city streets. Juxtaposed against this version of urban pastoral is the sharp awareness, offered from an adult perspective, that it was always difficult for a black man to keep any "original dream of America alive." Williams had become alienated from the American dream largely because of his experience during World War II. He had concluded sadly that "America had become a stranger to my earliest dreams" (5). Now, at the age of 38, Williams begins a four-month trip through America in order to take the national pulse and also to locate his identity as an American. "America was stirring as it had never stirred before. It was indeed a time in which to live, and a time to go" (6).

In *This Is My Country Too* (a title that was developed by a *Holiday* editor and which Williams does not like), the author measures his own psychic quest against racial realities in various regions of the country. Thus the narrative, informed by the loose structure typical of travelogs, moves across a series of social and geographical points. Starting from Syracuse, Williams proceeds to Vermont and New Hampshire. By plane, he goes from Boston to Detroit to pick up a car donated by Ford as part of the *Holiday* commission; then southward to Louisville, Nashville, Atlanta, Birmingham, New Orleans, and intermediate points, and back north to Chicago where the first half of the book ends. The second half chronicles his journey westward: his swing down to Los Angeles; the return across the Southwest and Midwest; Christmas in Syracuse with his two sons and divorced wife; a final rendezvous with his American destiny in Washington, D.C., the geopolitical center of everything that Williams was writing about and a fitting topographical conclusion for the book.

Williams's journey had psychic, political, and cultural implications that he suspected in advance, and which initially had made him reluctant to accept the assignment. For one thing, he knew that he would have to travel to the South at a time when the civil rights movement was eliciting murderous violence from entrenched segregationists in Dixie. Moreover, he suspected that he inevitably would have to trace an outline map of race relationships in the United States, but he did not want to emphasize this aspect of his travels. At the most visceral level, he knew that there might be a severe testing of his own identity, for he would be measuring his very manhood against a potentially lethal American landscape. In his foreword to the book, he asks: "Does a white American have to orient himself psychologically for some aimless wandering about the country? To a degree, yes, but not a great deal. For me some sort of psychological preparation was necessary. Eventually I became ready, but it was a costly process" (xix).

Williams knows what awaits him in his journey across America, and thus his quest assumes the overtones of a man seeking peace in a complex, violent, and disturbing world. The national environment does not provide peace even in the one city that Williams thought might not have changed, for in Syracuse an old classmate fails to recognize him in a restaurant. In Boston, another childhood friend, now a pimp, does recognize him but only to offer him a free girl as a symbol of status; other friends scattered across the United States have opted for security and the materialistic lures of the American dream. It is difficult for Williams to locate any sense of peace, even with personal friends, except when he is alone with America, enjoying the role of the solitary pilgrim swallowed in mountain or rural vastness, "striking out on another golden day" (12), enjoying the freedom to go.

Yet the movement of this contemporary explorer must of necessity be within American society. Unlike the original pioneers or fictive incarnations like Natty Bumppo, Williams cannot penetrate beyond society and civilization in his search for a promised land. Any peace or sense of harmony for him must be achieved with difficulty, and it will be the result of an assertion of manhood, a manifestation of grace under pressure. "I was not prepared to return from the South or anywhere else in America," Williams writes, "if it were put to me that I was less than a man, less than an Ameri-

can with more here than most, blood, bones, and sweat"
(37). Ready for combat with America and with himself, he asserts the need for pride, a willingness to sacrifice everything,
in the quest for a "sense of ownership in America."

Despite the notes of courage, hope, and optimism in *This
Is My Country Too*, the book essentially offers a critique of
American society in the 1960s. While Williams skirts the
other America, offering vivid sketches of poor blacks in the
South; and while he touches base with people of power, in
fluence, and celebrity, ranging from Ralph McGill, to Tommy
Davis, to Arthur Schlesinger, Jr.; he concentrates more on
the middle-class America that he knows best and that constitutes the source of greatest strength in his fiction. He offers
candid assessments of "Negro business" (owned often by
whites) in black sections of town; measures the black middle
class and its professional and social aspirations in cities like
Atlanta; paints a sad picture of the moral and political failures of black colleges in the South; exposes the residual
racism in the armed forces after a visit, one of the most vivid
parts of the narrative, to the Strategic Air Command base at
Grand Forks, North Dakota. Only occasionally does he in-
dulge in black local color, as in his discussion of the origins
of the "Kakewalk":

Negro slaves, spying from behind their cabins, saw the grand master's family going to church or to some other special affair. Since
the slaves knew the family intimately, the majestic airs displayed
on festive occasions were comical and hypocritical. At their own
clandestine affairs the slaves imitated the master and his family,
grossly caricaturing their way of walking, the twist of the shoulders, the swing of the arms. The slaves were caught and made to
perform, before white audiences, what master thought a purely
Negro dance. When the onlookers laughed at the Negroes strutting
and swinging, they were laughing at themselves. (16–17)

What Williams is far more interested in than local color is
whether contemporary versions of the cakewalk are still required. Here, as when he encounters an old black porter in a
Louisville hotel who insists on carrying the author's heavy
luggage all the way to the room, he discovers again that old
roles and images die hard—that assumed identities are still
needed for survival. The shops along Bourbon Street in New

Orleans still sell enormous Mammy dolls. There is still segregation in hotel accommodations, although Williams is denied a room only once. A cautious, confused mood is abroad in the land. As Hodding Carter tells Williams in one of several revealing interviews in the book, it is going to get worse before it gets better.

Carter, speaking to Williams in the early fall of 1963, was prophetic both in immediate and far-reaching terms. John Kennedy was assassinated while Williams was visiting his mother in Los Angeles. Suddenly the line of his travels—especially the movement from Syracuse to Hind County, Mississippi, where his mother grew up, to Los Angeles—and his quest for peace are shattered by the madness of political assassination. Williams and his family are moved emotionally by the murder, but with Los Angeles rife with the rumor that a black man had killed Kennedy, the author offers a more detached meditation, a coda of sorts for the entire book, on the fragility of the American dream:

I watched my family reach across generations of poverty and persecution and extend to the Kennedys deep and sincere sympathy. But a heavy air of irony remained, as if they had known all along that disaster, sickness, hate, and anarchy had to extend beyond them to encompass even the mightiest. . . . They knew that to be any degree black was to scream down the ages that the American dream at the beginning was not yet fulfilled, and that when the opportunity to fulfill it has been presented like the seats on a Ferris wheel, it has only been ignored. (121)

The weight of history, as well as the ambiguity of the American dream, accompanies Williams as he returns east. He is exhausted by the time he reaches Syracuse for Christmas with his sons, yet he pushes himself toward a final confrontation with the American dream in Washington, D.C., reflecting on the earlier March on Washington in which he had participated and on Martin Luther King's stirring invocation to the strength of the American dream. Williams acknowledges the continuing paradoxes of the dream, the difficulties involved in retaining a "vast share in America" (161). At the conclusion of _This Is My Country Too_, he asserts that he has searched for hope in America and located it in small pockets of love, friendship, concern and commitment: "I am committed to the search, the hope, the challenge, whether I want to be or not, for America has yet to sing its greatest songs" (162).

John Williams wrote an afterword one year after his journey around America and following four and a half months overseas. From this distance in time, his attempt to locate the promise of the American dream seems like a fleeting vision or perhaps just a literary exercise. Williams returned to the United States on the day that the three civil rights activists disappeared in Mississippi—a brutal episode that created a watershed in the author's own career. The afterword is a bitter reflection on the violence in our American origins; on slavery, oppression, and genocide, and on the bankruptcy of the political system. Americans, concludes Williams, are far from the ideal; they are virulent descendents of murderers and thieves who "had to be whipped out of filthy European jails and forced aboard flimsy vessels to journey here" (166). In the murder of John F. Kennedy and the violence resulting from the civil rights movement, Williams sees the specter of anarchy closing in on the land. If the American dream is to be celebrated, thinks Williams, Americans had better learn quickly a new and more inspiring song.

Throughout his nonfiction, which is a reflection of and testing board for his fiction, John Williams is alone with America, trying to decipher its riddles, mysteries, and paradoxes. He also seeks confirmation of some sustaining American spirit. He was on the road again in 1966 and 1967, exploring primarily this time black middle-class culture,[22] even as in the summer of 1967 there were rebellions in Newark and Detroit. His vision of America would intensify in its bleakness in the 1960s and early 1970s; and although the vision would moderate and become more temperate, it would never lose its critical edge. Nor would Williams cease his travels and his search for America, whether on the banks of the Potomac or in Plains, Georgia.[23] John Williams has observed that possibly history lies wrapped in the cocoon of ritual. In his nonfiction, as well as the fiction, he explores steadily those rituals that define the history of America—its collective and national destiny.

Chapter Three
American Dreams:
One for New York,
Night Song, and *Sissie*

There are three distinct phases to John Williams's career as a novelist. The first, embracing *One for New York, Night Song*, and *Sissie*, runs from 1956 to 1963; during this phase, the author worked at evolving an appropriate style and fictive structures, conveying a tone of cautious optimism in his depiction of possibly affirmative lives in America. The second phase in his progression as a novelist stretches from the mid-1960s to the publication of *Captain Blackman* in 1972. Reversing the spirit of affirmation and experimenting with new fictive forms, Williams erects in *The Man Who Cried I Am, Sons of Darkness, Sons of Light, and Captain Blackman* a world where the American dream vanishes, to be replaced by a world governed by unmanageable racial, historical, and political violence. The fiction of Williams's third phase, a product of the mid-1970s and 1980s, loses much of its political force in *Mothersill and the Foxes* and *The Junior Bachelor Society*, only to regain it in a highly autobiographical dimension in *!Click Song*. In tone and structure, the work of the third phase suggests a return to the spirit of affirmation, always achieved at cost and with sacrifice, found in the first stage.

If there is a basic idea animating Williams's first three novels, it is that of the American dream: its elusive quality; the forces of personal and institutional racism that thwart people seeking the dream; the ultimate capacity of individuals to move toward it, even to attain it in a significant way.

47

Each of these novels concentrates on strong, talented, intelligent, and tenacious people who resist the exploitation and oppression inherent in American society, who do not rebel militantly against that society (the only figure who does rebel—Eagle in *Night Song*—destroys himself), and who attain finally a measure of success or the promise of fulfillment. Critics have mistaken the general tone of "anger" in these novels, which is scarcely in the tradition of the "apologetic protest novel."[1] Anger is a convenient label that blurs the true tone of Williams's early fiction, which is essentially affirmative. Although he is not apologetic, he does not develop the hard edge of political protest that would characterize his three novels coming after *Sissie*. The characters in the early novels refuse to be exploited or degraded; they preserve themselves at all costs, and often those who are dearest to them. They struggle successfully to establish authentic lives.

One for New York

Williams's first novel, *One for New York*, was completed in 1956 but not published until 1960, after it had undergone five complete revisions. When it was brought out in January 1960 as an Ace Books paperback original, the editor had changed the title, with the author's reluctant consent, to *The Angry Ones.* "A better selling title," the editor had declared, and Williams, unaware that "angry" would become subsequently a label applied to himself and to his work, "mumbled agreement." As Williams noted, "I wanted the thing published."[2]

One for New York is not an unusually angry novel, or a complicated one in terms of plot or vision. Told simply in a straightforward, linear manner that carries the action through the summer, fall, and winter of one year in the mid-1950s, the novel traces the quest of Steve Hill, the protagonist, for purpose and stability in his personal and professional life. Hill is the first in a series of characters in Williams's fiction who is hounded by an elusive American dream. A publicist in his thirties who comes to New York from California to seek a job, Hill is bent on making it after several wasted years in "the peculiar American rat race."

What he seeks, in a broad and largely uncritical way, is a normal, middle-class existence, a modestly successful life:

I had it all planned. My dreams, the things I'd been working for, were to pay off in another five years. They were not elaborate dreams; I'd have a job I liked, and I'd grow in it, have security in it and be able to do other things when I had time. It was in essence quite a simple dream. There are in America many people for whom work they desire is achieved as a matter of course. They don't have to dream about it. But I had some doubts my dreams would come off. Still, dreams can be either the best or the worst things in the world to have. You're walking around dead if you don't dream.(5)

Sensing the disparity between the dream and the reality, Hill nevertheless commits himself to a series of vaguely defined goals. He is a survivor of World War II in the all-black Ninety-second Division, and the first in an American family descended from the Onondaga and the Ivory Coast Baule to hold a college degree. He believes that intelligence, skill, tenacity, and hard work will eventually pay off. Throughout the twenty-one episodic chapters, he learns that the dream tricks, corrupts, or devours most of the Americans who pursue it.

The landscape of _One for New York_ is filled with people, largely two-dimensional types, who dream of heroism, fame, love, family, success, and sexual fulfillment, but who invariably find their aspirations thwarted or destroyed. There is Grant, Steve's brother, "a steady unimaginative" (38) person who is killed in Korea, after having struggled to provide his wife Grace and his two children with "a home, a car, insurance, all that goes into what it takes to be secure in our time" (36). There is Grace herself, beautiful, warm, vibrant, who had been Steve's girlfriend, but who had been so obsessed with security that she had rejected him because of his uncertain vocation. Link and Bobbie Mason, Steve's college classmates, are succeeding in New York at the cost of their sanity and private lives. Obie Robertson, editor of _World of the Black_, is a long-standing friend of Steve's, who loses his job and finally commits suicide. There is Rollie Culver, homosexual editor of a vanity press who employs Steve only to exploit him, as he does all others. Hadrian Crispus, a southern redneck, dreams of becoming a successful author and is manipulated crudely by Culver. Lois Fleck is a lonely New York Jew who has an affair with Steve Hill, which founders on their mutual exploitation of each other. Basically, Hill is surrounded by psychological and societal casualties. He too has all the credentials of a victim, of another "one for New York" who will be destroyed by dreams. Hill is tested by New York, the center of a culture going rotten, but manages to survive, clinging to an uncertain but conceivably more authentic future.

The problem of authenticity besets many of the characters in Williams's works. As first-person narrator, Hill embodies the problem in several ways. In part, the question of authenticity hinges on the dilemma of "double consciousness" that Steve must live with, a psychological attitude initially investigated by W. E. B. DuBois, and one that is a major motif in black American writing.[3] Stated simply, Steve Hill is conscious of himself and also of the way that the white world perceives him, and this double rendering of self creates a growing split in his personality and in his ability to function. At the start of the novel, he thinks that a letter of introduction to officials at NBC might be sufficient to obtain a job that he knows he is qualified for. New York itself reflects his confidence:

New York has a way, when you catch it just right, of doing things to you, and I felt then that the city was doing something to me, for I began to admire its people, its buildings, its busyness. It was relatively cool. A haze softened the stark outlines of the midtown buildings and I had a great feeling of, not hope, but confidence.(10)

Hill does not get a job at NBC; the institutionalized racism, polite and urbane, that he encounters there is a prelude to the discrimination that he will encounter in personnel agencies, real estate firms, apartment complexes, and the publishing world. Racism in the 1950s is cool, subtle, effective. Hill, like everyone, exists in the world, but the world forces the central character to perceive himself in a certain way and to compromise his talents and his dreams.

Authenticity is also a dilemma in the vocational choice and commitments that Hill makes. Of necessity, he accommodates himself to the one job that he is able to obtain. When race and necessity are stripped away, however, the matter of work becomes an existential choice. At the outset, Hill is elated to be working. He hurls himself into activities at Culver's vanity press, working on canned reviews, manuscript reports, advertising and promotional copy. For him, work—any sort of work—conveys "some purpose in being" while unemployment results in uncertainty, depression, and fear. "Being without this—without a job, without something to do when you want to do something—is the worst thing in the world that can happen to you" (33). Gradually, however, Hill develops a more critical attitude toward the American work ethic. Having himself worked for a vanity press, the author knows how exploitative these operations are, and he conveys much of his own distaste through Steve Hill. One of the strengths of the novel is its systematic indictment of vanity publishing, which Williams depicts as a cannibalistic world where publishers feed on the dreams of ordinary people: "It made me angry that Rollie could be ruthless with people's dreams. Being a dreamer, I know how important, sometimes even more than life itself, dreams can be" (61). Yet Hill assumes complicity in an enterprise that becomes distasteful to him (unlike Obie, who becomes a fatality of the system) for he permits himself to be compromised. Obie's suicide and a series of violently unwinding relationships induce Hill at the end of the novel to quit his job and seek a more authentic one, recognizing fully that, as an honest employment counselor had told him, the task will not be an easy one.

The final level of authenticity that Hill must resolve is in his relationships with others. If he is not a fully sympathetic character, it is because of his limited sensibility, his inability to commit himself to people. Although capable of warmth and gregariousness, he is more often alienated, cynical, suspicious, and manipulative. His experience in the world has molded his defensive posture, but this attitude produces a limited or constricted personality. He has an innate distaste for Culver and his advances, yet in one instance he leads Culver on, only to turn on him violently after he has brought Culver to a state of sexual anticipation.

Sexual manipulation is also involved in Hill's affair with Lois Fleck, which begins immediately following his violent encounter with Rollie. There is a natural affinity between Lois and Steve and also a shared perception of ethnic and racial suffering. They break up each other's loneliness, yet there is something tenuous about their relationship. In a final confrontation scene, Steve says of their motivations: "You wanted revenge for the way your folks treated you. I wanted revenge for the way people treated me. We're even. Retaliation all around" (165). Sexual manipulation and sexual violence are variables in much of Williams's fiction, as well as emblems of inauthenticity. When toward the end of the novel, Link accuses Hill of having an affair with Bobbie and forces him to fight, the terms of sexual conflict, often with racial overtones, are starkly, perhaps melodramatically etched. Gradually, as people lapse into crazed or neurotic states of behavior, Steve finds that he has assumed complicity in their madness; however, he retains the will to struggle, the ability to reject finally what is false and to insist on his essential worth. He is the first man in Williams's fiction to cry "I am," which is the true reality at the end of his existential quest.

Toward the very end of the novel, Hill learns to identify with suffering when he sees Obie dying on a hospital stretcher. He experiences the horror of insanity that night in drunkenness and nightmare. Almost overwhelmed by conflicting emotions, he nevertheless emerges purged of the inauthentic impulses that were crippling him. He quits his job, avoiding the temptation to punish Rollie for his insults, knowing finally that people were as prepared to feed on his violence as on his talent or his sexuality. He calls Grace to propose marriage, and then phones Graff, the employment counselor, to begin his search for the right job.

Steve Hill derives from the many protagonists in American fiction for whom the world holds romantic promise. Traveling across America in the first chapter, reversing the movement of heroes from Natty Bumppo to Malamud's Levin in *A New Life*, Hill retains the ability to act on the basis of his dreams. Despite the sickness in American society, the violence in the American grain, the persistence of "the problem," or racism, he never loses completely his capacity for wonder. Toward the end of the novel he speculates, "I never thought my dreams could not come true. It would take a long time, maybe, and perhaps there would be moments when the visions would be obscured completely, but they'd come true" (143).

One for New York is an accomplished first novel but ultimately limited in scope, execution, and force. Although the first-person narrative permits Williams to create a portrait of a recognizable type of individual, Steve Hill remains a curiously wooden figure, a person whose inner moral and emotional life is never fully revealed to the reader. Williams would quickly abandon the first-person viewpoint, and move beyond stereotyping (the most egregious example in the novel is the clearly distasteful portrait of Rollie Culver) to the creation of characters who have well-defined roles and distinctive personal lives. What Williams would not abandon was his focus on major problems of life in America, on the tension between expectations and results. The incipient paranoia and violence in *One for New York* disappear at the end of the novel, replaced by a more positive vision of a man on the verge of authentic success. Gradually, Williams's tone would darken as his fiction moved toward its major phase. His perception of men and women and their relationship to social, political, and historical forces would also broaden and become more profound as he slowly developed the ideal fictive vehicles for his ideas.

Night Song

The characters in Williams's second novel, *Night Song* (1961), are not older than Steve Hill, but they have absorbed a deeper wisdom about life in America that parallels the author's evolving vision. *Night Song* is cast in dark urban shadows. Characters shamble or rush furiously through the night world of the novel, hurled uptown and downtown, from the Hudson to the East River, by a fierce winter wind that they seem unable to escape. It is a violent landscape, with the main personalities doing damage to others and to themselves. It is a lonely world where individuals struggle to make contact with one another. That any sort of affirmative vision emerges from this landscape is one of the interesting tonal features of *Night Song*, although Williams arrives at an affirmative statement more painfully, more equivocably, and at greater cost than he did in *One for New York*.

The genesis of *Night Song* can be traced to Williams's interest in the life of Charlie Parker. "In 1959, I think it was," Williams has written, "I got together with Bob Reisner who used to write a jazz column for the *Village Voice*, and we were going to do a nonfiction book on Bird. Bob already had a lot of material, and I collected more. Then we took the idea to Sam Vaughan, an editor at Doubleday, who toyed with the idea two or three weeks, finally turning it down."[4] What emerged ultimately was Williams's very fine appreciative essay, "Subject: Charlie Parker" and, more significantly, the archetypal figure of Eagle, patterned largely after Parker, in *Night Song*.

Charlie Parker's troubled life had mythic dimensions long before his death in New York on March 12, 1955. A legend in his personal life and in his music, Parker stands for, as Williams declares, "the slow erosion of an exceptional Negro symbolic of the assonances and dissonances that are America" (*Flashbacks*, 222). Bird, a jazz genius and magnetic personality, seemingly turned his short life into a modern portrait of the artist as rebel. A pariah for years among his musician colleagues and a subject of fascination and revulsion for America's jazz audience, Charlie Parker lived on the hard edge of nihilism. He haunted the placid postwar American decade, his wild form and revolutionary sounds emblematic of the darker impulses in the national experience of the time. Transformed into Eagle in *Night Song*, Charlie Parker animates the novel; his spirit colors the nocturnal jazz world that the main characters inhabit and informs major themes in the book.

Because of the presence of Eagle and the myths he embodies and because of the very ambiance of the novel, *Night Song* belongs to that minor category of American literature labeled "jazz fiction."[5] It is the best representative of this subgenre, but it would be wrong to treat it simply as a topical presentation of one aspect of American culture. Williams is an expert in the jazz idiom; he knows the subtleties of musical forms, the personalities who attach themselves to the jazz world, and the history of the movement itself. All this he captures with fidelity in *Night Song*; but the novel itself is not a limited offering of lives in a subculture or an atmospheric presentation of a small slice of life. In many ways imbued with archetypal overtones, *Night Song* is a blues piece whose strains reach into America's racial and ethnic core.

On the narrative level, the novel traces Richie "Eagle" Stokes's decline during the last few months of his life; the parallel decline of David Hillary, an unemployed alcoholic college professor, and his ambiguous movement back upward toward his former life; and the efforts of Keel Robinson, a preacher, who has been Eagle's mentor, to find himself and to create an enduring relationship with Della, a white social worker. The action is set largely in Greenwich Village, and centered on the coffee house that Keel runs as much as a refuge for musicians as in order to get by. Told from a shifting third-person point of view, the story successfully captures the interlocking worlds of these characters, their shared problems, and their essential conflicts. *Night Song* is one of Williams's most sustained accounts of racial interrelationships and of the difficulties involved in shedding racial and sexual roles for more authentic existences.

The book opens and ends with David Hillary, and although more of the novel is devoted to him than to the other two main characters, Eagle and Keel, he cannot be considered the protagonist. Basically, in fact, this is a novel without a central character, a narrative in which three types of individuals seem almost like allegorical figures in a contemporary urban hell. At the start of the novel, Hillary enters a pawn shop to hock his wedding ring in order to get money for liquor. Hounded by the death of his wife in an automobile accident that he might have caused, and with his academic career seemingly lost beyond retrieval, Hillary appears as a white pilgrim in a cold, dark, and alien world. He meets Eagle, who is pawning his saxophone, and soon finds himself being guided downtown, from bar to bar, by this frantic man with a "black, bloated face upon which some intense evil seemed to have traced its course."[6] Hillary's descent, his movement downtown to the Village, has symbolic implications. He enters a world where the presence of evil is stamped on every face. It is his burden to understand the source of that evil, to purge it from himself, and to find in a world that for him becomes not a hell but a refuge that holds the possibility of salvation. In the course of the novel, Hillary develops a limited capacity to care for Eagle and for Keel; but at a crucial stage in the action, he fails to offer aid to Eagle, who needs his help.

Eagle is an ambiguous and dangerous guide for anyone. Often high on liquor or heroin, unreliable and unpredictable in his behavior, Eagle is a vivid embodiment of a man burning down toward death. It is he who turns the night world of the novel into a paradigm of suffering for Hillary and a hectic maze for anyone trying to keep up with him. Eagle is cool and manipulative, especially toward the leeches who cling to the jazz world and who attempt to use him in turn. He makes love violently to the white women infatuated with jazz musicians, and he carries an aura of fierce destructive energy about him. He is a fighter, but his posture ultimately is a defensive one. The way he moves—in a "crouching, threatening walk"—is an index to his condition. Eagle's progress through the world, running "in that crouch in which one shoulder seemed pushed around in front of his body to ward off any blows that might come in his direction" (11), involves him in an unending series of physical and psychological violence. Much smarter than Hillary and infinitely more talented, Eagle has an innate sense of his futile condition. He knows the price he has had to pay for being a talented black man in America. He is angered and saddened by this knowledge and gradually he is worn down by it. Talking to Hillary, who had helped to save him from dying from a drug overdose, he explains the raw elements of his condition:

His face was dull with a sadness which startled Hillary, but he didn't interrupt the silence. "I guess I was damned near gone last night," Eagle said at last. "Any night will do. I'm tired. I'm tired of things in this land: kids tryin' to go to school, shysters all over you, phonies ass-hole deep—" He heaved in his chair but still did not turn away from the room. "I'm so tired of so many things, but goddam if I'll quit." (73–74)

Eagle knows his condition, and turns his music and his rebellious posture into a cry against it. He lets himself burn out, registering his sadness and disdain for America in the process.

Night Song in many ways is about varieties of exhaustion. Eagle's exhaustion is elemental, the result of his artistic and personal battles with a hostile nation. Hillary's exhaustion, from which he partially recovers, is banal, a sign finally of moral weakness. The exhaustion Keel Robinson feels is the most complex in the novel and derives from his attempt to administer to the suffering of the world, to bridge the white and black realms through his relationship with Della, and to find a genuinely authentic calling for himself. Although Keel does not stride across the pages of *Night Song* with the magic and animus with which Williams invests Eagle, he gradually takes hold of the reader's imagination, and in many ways remains both the most well-rounded and engaging figure in the book. Unlike either Eagle or Hillary, he assumes responsibility for the maintenance of a moral universe and for those whose moral bearings and whose very lives have been damaged. He recognizes Eagle's frustrated genius and his dilemma, and he cares for him. He employs Hillary in his coffee house, offering the drunken academician a chance to emerge from self-pity. As he declares early in the novel, "I don't know why a white man can't make it in society" (17). He absorbs Hillary's latent hostility toward him and tries to turn it toward brotherhood. He does not give up his relationship with Della, although things have not been going well between them for quite some time.

Keel, a Harvard seminarian and former preacher, simply quit his calling, as he did his conversion to Islam, because it was not the authentic thing for him. He remains, however, a deeply religious and most profoundly committed figure. He is one primary figure in Williams's fiction who is not beguiled by the garish outlines of the American dream, who knows early on that the contours of success are not economic or even secular, but based on bonds between people. His proprietorship of the coffee house enables him to get by and also to offer, through the maintenance of a Musician's Room in the restaurant, a haven for jazz players. Keel gets by, having abandoned an earlier impulse to "make a living." Simplifying his economic needs, he concentrates on the ef-

fort to erect a small world, a private microcosm that is based
on life-sustaining forces, rather than the self-destructive ones
that circulate around Eagle and Hillary. Unlike Eagle and
Hillary, Keel has an ability to quit what is bad for him and to
sustain, even in anguish, possibilities that are good.

Keel's world is the same as Eagle's, the same as the world
that Hillary has adopted at least for a time, but he alone lo-
cates meaning in it:

> It was there, in the world of cool, that he had met Della, there in
> that world of arrogant musicians and worrying nightclub owners,
> a world filled with admirers, detractors, tourists, hipsters, squares,
> policemen, and weirdies, a world in which the days were really
> nights because you lived mostly in the dark and sang your song of
> life then. There had been instant communication between them
> and no little grappling with the things both had learned at other ex-
> tremes of their lives. (54)

Keel, however, also feels the coldness and exhaustion of the
world, and he has been rendered sexually impotent by it.
Slowly he overcomes the impotence and works through his
agonies to a point where marriage with Della is a possibility.
What he knows about existence is distilled into his criticism
of Hillary toward the end of the novel, after Hillary has confessed that he refused to help when Eagle was being beaten
up by a cop in the same upstate New York college town
where they had planned to rendezvous, Eagle on tour, and
Hillary reapplying for a teaching post. Keel says to Hillary:

> "You owed Eagle nothing, I guess. Even if he did give you money,
> his bed, his food, and yes, love. Eagle has love. You could never
> understand: you still look in the sky—yes, you do,—for God,
> when God is people, has always been people and that's where
> Eagle looks; where else would a man with sense look?" (193)

Keel is no simpleminded Samaritan. He suffers himself, and
feels anger and hatred. Yet he never loses his capacity for
charity, for *caritas*—the ability to feel for others. He and
Della, who is also without illusion, carry with them the affirmative spirit of the novel. By the end of *Night Song*, Eagle is
dead of an overdose, while Hillary, heading out of the cool

world toward a summer teaching assignment, is a more equivocal figure: "Someday Hillary would understand. Maybe. The bus edged through the toll booths, down the brick road into the gaping mouth of the tunnel' (219). The symbolism in the last lines of *Night Song*, as well as Williams's editorializing, intimate that Hillary's pilgrimage is not at an end and that he must learn much more about himself and about the world before he is transformed by the capacity to love.

This novel represents a considerable advance by Williams over his first one. His style is more certain and his fictive canvas is populated with characters, major and minor, whose personalities and behavior Williams probes with skill. Narrative movement is swift, and key themes are consistently dramatized rather than presented in a prescriptive manner. *Night Song* is not a protest novel in the traditional sense, but rather a sensitive presentation of a special landscape, a night-time world populated by musicians and others attached to them, and of the struggles of people to locate some life-sustaining meaning in it. Williams never permits the metaphorical or symbolic overtones attached to this world and to the characters' quests in it to become obtrusive or to operate against the concrete presentation of personality. He looks very carefully at characters, developing them in all their complexity and refusing either to glorify or demean any of them. In a topical sense, Williams erects in *Night Song* the essentially black world of jazz musicians better than any other American writer.

In a more significant way, the black world that he orchestrates, a world that functions in the context of a broader and predominately white society, serves Williams as preparation for the creation of a much deeper world of black Americans in his next novel, *Sissie*. He does not declare his anger in *Night Song* over the frustration of black talent, the exploitation of artists, the difficulty of sustaining black-white relationships, and the racism that brings people up against cold urban walls; instead, he successfully contrives to have his four main characters embody these ideas in their actions. At the end of *Night Song*, Eagle's self-destructive journey is finished. Hillary, presented more sympathetically in the first half of the novel than in the second, has failed in several key symbolic tests, and in one way or the other had managed to compromise or defile his relationships with Eagle, Keel, and Della; his journey toward fulfillment remains uncertain. Keel and Della, however, have worked through their problems; they have kept the faith with each other, not without considerable pain, and they remain at the core of meaning in *Night Song*. Together, they represent Williams's creation of an affirmative spirit that is more convincing than the vague optimistic glow at the end of his first novel. There has been death in *Night Song*, as well as exhaustion and waste. The very landscape of New York seems to oppress people. Beyond this, Williams implies that there is a code in the world separating people that individuals must overcome. What people learn they must communicate to each other. Art, the music of Richie Stokes, is significant, but not enough. Learning, the desiccated presentation of facts that Professor Hillary is capable of, also is not sufficient. Total commitment to other lives is needed, and it is this sort of commitment, seen in Keel and Della, that flickers throughout *Night Song* and lingers at its end.

Sissie

Williams's third novel, *Sissie*, which he began in 1960 and saw published in 1963, elaborates themes found in his earlier fiction. Here we see the ongoing struggle of individuals to succeed, to contain anger and violence, and to resolve the struggle in creative ways. We detect a tone of hope emerging from the troubled lives of the characters. *Sissie*, however, is more important for its departures than for its continuities in terms of Williams's evolving craft and vision. It is remarkable, unique in its handling of subject matter, far more sophisticated than the first two novels in method and filled with stylistic strengths and subtleties that indicate an author emerging as a strong and significant artist. *Sissie* presents, for the first time in Williams's career, a self-contained world of black experience on which the larger world can impinge but which it can never affect in terms of deep structure. Unlike the situation in the first two novels, black-white relationships are kept at the periphery. As a homage to the black family, Williams tries to keep the black world inviolate, even as the omnipresent white world can never disappear. Characters in *Sissie* do not exist as isolated figures, but as part of a communal fabric. This shift in perception, involving the presentation of a culture of cohesiveness and integrity, is not seen again in Williams's fiction until the publication of a much later novel, *The Junior Bachelor Society*.

Sissie is the story of a black American family, the Joplins. It is plotted in four parts and ranges historically and culturally from the 1920s to the early 1960s. As fiction, the novel offers corrective adjustments to earlier sociological studies of the black family by writers like Frazier and Franklin. These studies tended to concentrate on the weakness and dissolution of the black family, a trend that was to be brought to extreme conclusion in Daniel Moynihan's *The Negro Family in America* (1965), where the author invented a "tangle of pathology" to characterize the family life of twenty million black Americans. As a novel of ideas about the black family, *Sissie* offers a complex and constantly dramatized account of a family that survives economic hardships, departures, and deaths, and that retains an essential spirit of vitality, an organic bond of blood. It is a novel of reverence and of wonder, conceivably the finest novel about its subject in American literature.

In the preface written especially for the 1969 Anchor edition of *Sissie*, Williams provides his own sociological introduction to the novel. Alluding to the deleterious effects of the Moynihan report and ignoring perhaps the inconsistencies of black sociologists, Williams constructs his own convincing thesis on the strength and vitality of black American families:

That black people in this nation have been capable of maintaining *any* family structure at all is so incredible a feat that it cannot be measured. The centuries of slave trade and slavery, if they were to be profitable to the fullest degree, as well as effective, did not dare to sustain the tribe, the group, the family. They were systematically destroyed except in rare, very rare cases. In such an atmosphere, I would think that the instinct to be a part of or to raise a family would have been bred out, beaten out, slaved out, but it was not.[7]

Williams has an innate personal grasp of what Herbert Gutman in his fine revisionist study, *The Black Family in Slavery and Freedom, 1750–1925*, documents convincingly as the cohesiveness of the black family despite the most vigorous assaults on its identity. "I came to this knowledge as a young man," Williams writes, "and for a long time I wanted to sing of this triumph, for that is precisely what it is. . . . In just over one century the black American family, still tattered and battered, has come back. That human triumph cannot be sung loudly enough" (vii-viii).

Williams constructs his song to the black family in counterpoint, using each of the four major parts of *Sissie* to present the Joplin family experience through different sets of eyes. In Part 1, the central consciousness is Sissie's grown daughter Iris, a famous singer who has established her reputation in Europe and who is now returning to her mother's sickbed after years of expatriation. Part 2 focuses on Ralph, Jr., Sissie's sole surviving son, who has carved a reputation in New York as a successful playwright. Part 3 tends to have a dual focus, concentrating first on Sissie, and then on her husband, Big Ralph. Part 4, the shortest section, assembles the characters at the Los Angeles hospital where Sissie dies. In each section, action moves on two time planes: a highly concentrated present time in late December that takes Iris and Ralph from New York to Los Angeles in approximately forty-eight hours; and a looser chronology, presented through multiple flashbacks of family history and, to a lesser degree, of national history (much like the scheme in the first section of Saul Bellow's *Herzog*). Williams elects to present this overlapping time scheme through the consciousnesses of several major characters, each possessing his or her own knowledge, shared experience, and individual perceptions. Thus we often come to an event more than once. What emerges is an exceedingly complex family chronology, somewhat confusing at the start but becoming clearer once the novel has been completed and, desirably, reread. On balance, Williams displays firm technical control of this method—a structural format that he would employ again, with greater success because of the focus on one central character rather than several, in his next novel, *The Man Who Cried I Am*.

A major advantage in Williams's decision to create successive central consciousnesses in *Sissie* (somewhat in the manner of Faulkner's *The Sound and the Fury*) is that he can
present both uniquely realized main characters as well as a
composite family group. Williams displays here a feeling for
the inner lives of his characters and a stylistic ability to
render personality graphically that transcends the considerable talents evident in his first two novels. In *Sissie*, character
evolves slowly, through long sinuous flashbacks involving
not just one central consciousness, but also others as they
reflect on the lives of family members. Iris and Ralph, who
channel their creative impulses into music and writing, are
intense studies of personalities evolving from childhood to
adulthood. Even characters to whom less attention is devoted—notably Big Ralph, whom we see only sporadically;
and Time, who played piano in Iris's group and from whom
she is now separated after a long affair—have a distinctness
of form indicating growth in the author's talents. As for
Sissie, whose actual appearance Williams delays more than
half the novel, there are elements in her characterization that
are unusually fine and complex.

We first learn about Sissie through the perceptions of Iris
and Ralph, both of whom (notably Iris) have had difficulty
coming to terms with her. Although separated from their
mother for years, they sense her as a presence in their lives,
subtly shaping their attitudes, molding their resilience, creating their drives, and instilling in them an ability to resist adversity. Presented from this dual perspective, she becomes a
significant force long before Williams devotes the first half
of the third part to her. She is not, however, a stereotyped
black mother. As Williams writes in his preface:

The white man and his social system, his life style, created the image of the black matriarch, the woman who runs the house in the
absence, real or psychological, of the man. Sissie could not be such
a stern, sexless, humorless creature. She is vengeful, cunning, and
often a fool. She is human and the white image of the matriarch
was not. Besides, I've known no black female head of a house who
did not bemoan the absence of the male, and not for sex alone, but
to provide the necessary discipline for raising black children in the
society. (ix)

Sissie is not a woman easily loved or understood by her children. Iris and Ralph require perspective, the relative security of success, and a basic understanding of history to appreciate their mother and accept the hard edges of her nature. The first image of Sissie is of a battler, a person who has struggled and persevered in an often unkind and harsh environment, a woman "never giving up, making small of whatever happened of her" (6–7). Sissie has survived the deaths of two daughters, Juanita and Mary Ellen, in infancy and early childhood; the Depression; poverty and welfare; and the death of her son, Robbie, in the Korean War. In later years, married a second time to Oliver and living in California, she has experienced her own worldly success and the larger successes of her two surviving children. In short, Sissie has survived the social traumas of twentieth-century American history, journeying from the deep South to an upstate New York city, Bloodfield (patterned after Williams's Syracuse), where she works most of her life as a maid, molded by social and economic currents as diverse as the Volstead Act and the accelerating rush of Americans to California in the 1950s. Williams is no longer content with depicting people in the present, which had been largely his procedure in *One for New York* and *Night Song*. Here he broadens and deepens his novel to capture Sissie, her husband Ralph, and her children in the web of history. Essentially, historical cross-currents are subordinated to the unique lives of the characters, molding them in unobtrusive ways. After *Sissie*, Williams would move more deeply into the writing of major historical fiction.

His expanding historical consciousness and growing technical ability permit him to generate in *Sissie* a sense of place, time, and character, as well as the impact of landscape on the lives of the Joplin family. Better than any sociological study, Williams's novel re-creates the black community, especially in the late 1920s and 1930s, with a stylistic precision and intensity that clearly shows the evolution of character under the impact of environment. There is no naturalistic simplicity or stylistic crudity in this presentation, but instead terse, controlled writing, a sustained account of the ways the black community adjusts to the larger world, of the limitations in the powers of adjustment, and of the inevitable constriction of lives because of racism and its attendant economic oppression, as well as the general condition of the times. The young Sissie has journeyed northward on a dirty, soot-filled Jim Crow car and finds herself employed by a white family that is not tyrannical but simply careless and uncaring in its assumptions about race. Nevertheless, she harbors dreams of a better life and of a happy marriage to Big Ralph, a popular, well-known singer:

> Well, she and Big Ralph had been sure they'd get out of Bloodfield, but they hadn't quite made it. The flat they lived in after they married was at least out of earshot of the can company, but the railroad tracks that ran down the main street of Bloodfield were inevitably there. Their flat was on the first floor and was approached along an upfaulting sidewalk and across an open wooden porch. The one light that entered the rooms came from the streetside windows; the rooms to the rear were oppressively gloomy. The furniture was maple. Linoleum covered all the floors. (157)

Bloodfield, a name suggesting the violence in people's lives and the violence done by environment to those lives, is a self-contained universe from which the escape envisioned by Sissie is elusive and normally impossible. Although she and Big Ralph both work hard, employment is always uncertain and events capricious. Gradually, they are worn down by successive traumas, many as natural as the weather itself: "The winter Juanita was born the temperature didn't rise above twenty degrees. First the coal gave out, and then the wood. Coke was cheap but gave little heat. Sissie would sometimes get into bed with the baby and Little Ralph while Big Ralph trudged through the snow to Jewtown to buy a sack of hard coal with borrowed money" (163). A chill affecting the lives of the Joplin family hangs over *Sissie*. The motif, which Williams establishes at the start of the novel as Iris flies into a biting New York winter, helps to identify the growing paralysis of possibilities for Sissie and her family.

Whether it is the death of Juanita or the callous and unwittingly scornful behavior of employers, there is a violence done to Sissie and to her family that slowly forces a self-consuming reaction. Sissie apprehends the reduction of her life, translating accurately the images coming to her from an alien environment. Making the bed of her employers, the Geigers, she wonders at the way they lay out intimate aspects of their lives for her: "She approached the bed; it smelled like stale bread. With tentative fingers she smoothed around the spots and fluffed the pillows. She could not understand why Mrs. Geiger didn't make the bed herself. Didn't she care if Sissie saw the spots? For a moment Sissie felt uneasy; she was an uncaring machine, a thing without substance, if the Geigers didn't care she knew; it was as if she didn't exist or as if she were invisible, but able, nonetheless to do their bidding" (153). Sissie's life is infected by the symbolic stains, just as Nancy, in Faulkner's celebrated story, "That Evening Sun," must carry the dirty laundry for the white community. For Big Ralph, once he loses his job as a singer, the violence of institutionalized racism is harsher. Ralph takes any job he can find, and with Sissie also working they manage to move to Jewtown, but the economic crash of 1929 brings a deeper bleakness to Ralph's life. Forced to work in the toilets at the state fair, Big Ralph must lapse into servility in order to receive tips from the customers. Conscious of the sacrifice in pride he has made so that he can provide for his family, he nevertheless retains the will to struggle, to keep his own identity and the family's identity intact. Yet even the natural world turns hostile. In a sequence that Williams derives from *Native Son*, the Joplin's flat is invaded by rats and roaches, until one day Big Ralph must kill a rat that had been nibbling at Iris's cheek. Each attempt to succeed seems to be neutralized by a countervailing destructive force. Big Ralph gets a WPA job, but that autumn Mary Ellen contracts pneumonia and dies. Shortly thereafter, Big Ralph leaves. Sissie systematically destroys all traces of him and takes on a succession of lovers.

Whereas the violence in Williams's first two novels had been highly stylized and occasionally melodramatic, when it appears in *Sissie* it is organic to the lives of the Joplins. Much of it seems overt and visceral, as when Ralph cuts Sissie's throat after learning of her affair with a man named Albert or when Sissie administers beatings to Ralph, Jr. Yet its causes are racial, cultural, and institutional. The psychological effects of constant poverty and ghettoization, as well as the demoralization stemming from the constant frustration of trying to sustain a family in adversity, create in Sissie especially a need for emotional release. This manifests itself in her habitual beatings of Ralph and her cool disdain of Iris, whom she uses as a foil against Big Ralph, telling him erroneously that Iris is Albert's daughter. Violence is a manifestation of Sissie's anger and frustration, and it is also a weapon that she uses not so much to victimize her children as to make them tough and resolute. Williams writes in his introduction to *Sissie*:

Black parents are much like parents anywhere. They love their children as much as any others; they worry about them. But because they are black the parental burden is greater. With what sometimes appears to be unbearable cruelty, they train their children to survive and even function in the hostile society into which they're born. In the loving then, there is hurt and in the hurting love." (ix–x)

Williams's evolving perception that the world itself is governed by violence and by megalomaniacal gnomes "who inhabited the secret control rooms of the world" (135) would become an overriding preoccupation for him in his subsequent three novels.

Sissie's surviving children are steeled for the world by their mother's sternness, but at a cost that must be measured in terms of hatred and the relative abilities of Iris and Ralph to resolve ambivalent feelings toward their mother. Brother and sister are in their thirties in the present action of the novel, and both are successes in their creative fields. Iris, after a disastrous marriage to a soldier, finds salvation in music and fame as a singer in Europe. The first of Williams's expatriates, she comes into contact with other Africans and Arabs, sensing in them a change in history: "When she and Time listened to them they exuded the sense that all of Europe had died and only Africa, her deserts and savannas and mountains and jungles lived and would be free of the French and the British" (66). Likened to Josephine Baker, Iris fits comfortably into the world of other black expatriate musicians and enjoys the adulation of European jazz crowds. Yet there is a streak of toughness in her, a latent suspicion of human relationships. She is alienated from her mother, from men (she loves Time but ultimately rejects him), and in a broader sense from America. Her return home at a time of family crisis fills her with nostalgia and with affection for Ralph, Jr., and his second wife, Eve. At her mother's death-bed, however, she refuses to forgive. As she tells Ralph moments after Sissie has died, "Ralph, it was the only thing she ever gave me besides clothes and food—the right to refuse" (226). Iris has her mother's resilience as well as her own creative gifts. Williams intimates at the conclusion of the novel that she will learn larger and more humane truths.

Ralph, Jr., has been a closer spectator than his sister of the tensions and disruptions in Joplin family life and has been in many ways more scarred by the experience. His resistance and his hatred are fueled by Sissie's own anger and frustration, as in the following sequence:

Once, when little Ralph had forgotten what he was to get at the store and returned with the wrong things, Sissie snatched up the leather belt. As she whipped him, she lost all sense of time and of reality; the strap snarled through the air again and again. "Cry, damn you," Sissie hissed, her breath growing short. When she saw the hatred in his eyes she beat harder. (186)

Violence in *Sissie* tends to feed upon itself. It is not exaggerated by Williams and is counterbalanced by warmer family emotions, notably a moving series of vignettes involving Big Ralph and his Little Ralph. At the same time, the family problems that manifest themselves in terms of aggression have an impact on all the Joplins. Ralph grows up hating his mother for the beatings. His adult life, however, is framed by a much darker recognition, that the internal family violence might have been caused by larger societal forces.

Sissie certainly sees enough of the white world and dreams of sharing in its relative riches, but it is Ralph, Jr., who develops severe problems concerning his ability to function in it. While in the Navy during World War II, Ralph kills a white man, Doughnut, who has baited him mercilessly and beaten him. Later, as Ralph struggles to survive and to succeed in

New York, the memory of Doughnut hounds him, becoming the symbol of fate. Ralph enters analysis largely because of the nightmares caused by this white face of fate and the constriction in creativity that he feels. The chapters devoted to Ralph's year of analysis are perhaps the least successful in the novel, not because they lack verisimilitude, but because there is a blurring in tone and a fluctuation in point of view that does not occur in other parts of *Sissie*.[8] As Ralph works his way through analysis, it is difficult to determine if Williams is parodying the experience or treating it objectively. Moreover, although the author succeeds in rendering the analyst, Dr. Bluman, in relatively sympathetic tones, the doctor tends to remain a stock type, the only one in the novel, limited in his perception of Ralph's dilemma. The successful sale of Ralph's play script induces him to give up analysis, and his own perception of violence and the relative enjoyment coming from it really has nothing to do with analysis: "violence was basic; it was always there, expected, met, bested if possible" (133). Ralph comes to terms with the violent contours of his life: "The family had understood the nature of violence even as they were being shipped from West Africa aboard, perhaps, the *Desire*, 120 tons, out of Rhode Island with its stink of slopping feces, urine, vomit, rotting bodies and stale bread" (133). Ralph understands his heritage better than Dr. Bluman ever can, and turns the violence to creative use through the power of art.

Despite the welter of disruptive forces in their lives, the surviving Joplins emerge as warm, loving people. One of the truly sensitive aspects of *Sissie* is Williams's ability to create this human bond of affection and of shared experience over and above the problems in their lives. Williams deals ultimately with the strengths of black families. Sissie herself, in a letter to Iris, telling her of the death of Robbie, uses a metaphor that suggests the assaults on family strength: "Lord, I wanted this family to be a great strong tree, like some of those oaks on your grampa's place. But something is eating that tree from the leaves and branches right down to the roots" (63). Nevertheless, the Joplin family survives, prospers, triumphs. "Survival," writes Williams in his introduction, "has always been the main business of black families on

these shores: that hasn't changed much in all the centuries"
(viii). Aside from pure survival, Sissie conveys both truths
and strengths to her children. She and both her husbands
work hard all their lives in order to avoid economic annihilation; her own aspirations infect her children; she instills in
them an ability to adapt to a hostile environment, and
ultimately to care for each other.

In *Sissie*, Williams punctures traditional myths about the
black American family. Sissie is no two-dimensional matriarch, nor are Iris and Ralph stereotyped, dysfunctional off-
spring of a broken family. Kinship remains strong, even as
Williams refuses to gloss over the anguish of the Joplins'
lives. Williams captures what Ralph Ellison once called
"'that something else,' that challenges the sociologists who
ignore it, and the society which would deny its existence. It
is 'that something else' which makes for our endurance and
our promise."[9] Williams draws family portraits that transcend sociological style and most sociological insights into
black family life in America. With subtlety, force, craftsmanship, and love, he fashions in *Sissie* a novel that serves as a
testament to a family that functions, that is creative, and that
endures.

Between the publication of *One for New York* in 1960 and
Sissie in 1963, John Williams arrived as a talented novelist.
His early novels during the decade of the 1960s operate on
hope, revealing how the destructive forces close to the bedrock of the American experience can be channeled into creative and life-sustaining paths by resolute people. His main
characters reject violence and tend to ignore history and
politics, even as they concentrate on their own condition,
which is governed ultimately by those forces they prefer not
to think about. Williams's world in the fiction of his first
phase is, then, largely apolitical. Yet he begins in *Sissie* to
scrutinize lives against the backdrop of history, and to
evolve increasingly more complicated fictive forms to place
characters within a historical dimension. *Sissie* is the land-
mark novel of Williams's first phase, a work of considerable
force and importance. But that self-contained world, filled
with promise for Sissie's surviving children, would vanish as
Williams and America moved deeper into the 1960s.

Chapter Four
Resistance, Rebellion, and Death: *The Man Who Cried I Am*

Four years elapsed between the publication of *Sissie* and Williams's fourth novel, *The Man Who Cried I Am*, released by Little, Brown in the fall of 1967. During this period, Williams traveled across the United States on assignment for *Holiday*; visited Mexico, Europe, Israel, and Cyprus; and covered Africa on assignment for *Newsweek*. Speaking of the evolution of *The Man Who Cried I Am* in 1981, Williams said: "I can remember writing part of the novel during the marches, when everybody got beat up. And I can remember working on it in Mexico, Spain, and Amsterdam." Williams spent three and a half years writing the novel, which is as international in scope as his own wanderings and, as a direct consequence of those travels and the political traumas of the times, considerably broader in conception than the three earlier novels. Alluding to Little Rock, Williams observed, "I guess that at that point I stopped being as unconcerned with direct political consequences as I had been with the first three books, and became concerned with the possibility that more terrible things could happen." Moreover, as a black man traveling around Europe and Africa, Williams became aware of the watchfulness of the U. S. government, and specifically the CIA.

The publication of *The Man Who Cried I Am* was accompanied by a relatively strong advertising campaign designed

71

in part as a challenge to the novel's main competition that
year, *The Confessions of Nat Turner*. Styron's novel received front-page reviews and sold exceptionally well. *The
Man Who Cried I Am*, relegated to other pages, had a generally favorable critical reception but modest sales.[1] Reviewers
did not seem to appreciate Williams's radical departure from
the more temperate vision implicit in his first three novels;
moreover, a few felt that the action of the new book was
somewhat implausible. Yet in retrospect, *The Man Who
Cried I Am*, with its militant social and historical prophecies,
is one of the most significant political novels of the American
1960s.

The Web of History

The Man Who Cried I Am is a bleak prediction for society.
International in its frame of reference, it traces a single man's
life and his relationships from the Depression to the 1960s.
Opening in Amsterdam in May 1964, the novel telescopes
modern history and centuries of historical consciousness
into the last day of Max Reddick's life. Reddick, suffering
from the final stages of rectal cancer, is a novelist and journalist whose vocation has forced him to record contemporary history. In fact, he is the incarnation of modern
historical horrors—a man literally sickened unto death by
history. In his final twenty-four hours, Reddick carries with
him the burden of contemporary history and ultimately, one
of its most terrifying secrets. By the end of the novel,
Reddick is dead, not from the cancer but rather from capricious historical forces that ironically come full circle.

Whereas John Williams's first three novels had contained
no overt political vision and had sought strategies for moving beyond violence and anger toward tentative affirmations
of social harmony, *The Man Who Cried I Am* is governed by
a radical historical consciousness. No longer content with
rendering the sociology of the black experience or hoping
for peaceful change, this novel is written in keeping with the
rage of the times. Lives are tenuous and atomistic. All apolitical temptations, as Irving Howe has called them—love, faith,
honesty, trust—are useless before the crushing political evil

of our times. Max Reddick, returning to Europe out of love for his ex-wife and honor for a dead friend, winds up dead himself. As the novel ends, Margrit Reddick waits for her former husband in an Amsterdam cafe, even orders a Pernod for him, not knowing that she is waiting for a ghost. Even in springtime, the world in *The Man Who Cried I Am* seems to suffer from exhaustion.

Williams began writing this work in 1964, at a time when his travels for the *Holiday* article had left him with serious misgivings abut the nation's social health.[2] He was still bothered by the 1962 scandal created by the American Academy in Rome, an incident that he would incorporate into the novel. More significantly, he had become preoccupied with the increasing violence, racial polarization, and cultural and political breakdown of the 1960s. In an interview, Williams mentioned that a critical moment in the evolution of his own political convictions came when the bodies of the three murdered civil rights workers were found in Mississippi on August 5, 1964. Subsequently, Williams would chronicle in three major novels of his second phase—*The Man Who Cried I Am*, *Sons of Darkness, Sons of Light*, and *Captain Blackman*—the failure of the United States to fulfill its historical promise. His fiction would become a literature in opposition to the defects he perceived in American culture. Focusing on political assassinations, urban conflagrations, and imperialistic wars, prophesying racial genocide, his trilogy of political novels would constitute a contemporary *U.S.A.* unmatched in quality and importance in the fiction of the past twenty years.

New fictive strategies and structures were needed to convey his political ideas as they developed during the 1960s and into the early 1970s. For *The Man Who Cried I Am*, he devised a form that permitted him to dramatize the lives of individuals caught in the web of history. Basically the narrative moves concurrently within two time frames. One is determined by the last hours of Reddick's life; the other extends over his reveries during this period. The first takes Max Reddick from his last meeting with Margrit to Leiden, where he picks up from the mistress of his deceased friend Harry Ames a volatile series of documents relating to the King

Alfred Plan (an international scenario for the incarceration of 20,000,000 black Americans in the event of civil war), to Reddick's liquidation by two CIA operatives on the road back to Amsterdam. Reddick, who is a terminal figure, a burnt-out case, also sees during this period his entire life unfold before him in what amounts to a prolonged day of death. Ultimately, the present and the past fuse: Max not only relives the past, but in his final twenty-four comes to terms with what he is, what of necessity he has been, and what he must do with the information left for him, as both personal curse (for Reddick had once slept with Harry Ames's wife) and political test, by his friend, mentor, and prime literary competitor.

In *The Man Who Cried I Am*, Williams presents and orchestrates numerous unique characters; yet at the same time, he clearly intends them to be more generalized types molded by race, sex, class, culture, economics, and most critically, politics. At the center of this dual approach to characterization is Max Reddick, a vividly realized individual who also functions as a symbol, a form of historical man. As a figure who personifies a historical and racial destiny, he tends to embody cultural patterns and events. We find him representative of more than thirty years of New York literary history (almost half the novel's twenty-nine chapters are set in this metropolitan area), as well as a history of black expatriation. We read in him a psychohistory of sexual relationships between the races, from the time in the late 1930s when black artists were encouraged in the fashionable pursuit of white women to a more recent era when interracial marriage is one apolitical alternative that glows like a fragile possibility. We read through his personal history of the broad contours of contemporary history—the Second World War, the 1948 Wallace campaign, the McCarthy trials, the Korean War, the emergence of independent African nations, the "New Frontier," the bus boycotts, marches, and church burnings, and the rise of new American leaders in the 1960s who, like Max Reddick, would become historical victims themselves. Possessing the broad geographic setting of three continents—America, Europe, Africa, *The Man Who Cried I Am* is Williams's critique of a world, indeed of an epoch, governed by malignant historical forces.

It is important to understand and appreciate the way that Williams renders history and projects a clearly delineated historical consciousness in *The Man Who Cried I Am*, for the novel is historical fiction in the best sense of the word. Unlike Capote in *In Cold Blood* or Mailer in *The Armies of the Night*, Williams does not attempt to apply novelistic techniques to a single historical episode. Nor does a historical figure serve as the prime character in his novel, as in Styron's *The Confessions of Nat Turner.* Moreover, although there are grotesque elements in Williams's novel, he does not attempt involuted historical fiction in the manner of Colombian author Garcia Marquez's *One Hundred Years of Solitude*, Pynchon's *V*, or Vonnegut's *Slaughterhouse Five.* Williams shares with all these writers a cynical attitude toward history, as well as a perception of its apocalyptic elements.[3] Yet his historical imagination is essentially more tragic than that of any of his contemporaries; while his method, relying on sophisticated flashback technique and reminiscent in certain ways of the experimental devices of documentary realism perfected by Dos Passos, owes a larger debt to more traditional forms of historical fiction. In *The Man Who Cried I Am*, Williams projects, as Georg Lukács writes, a world where "crises in the personal destinies of a number of human beings coincide and interweave within the determining context of an historical crisis."[4] The historical crisis in this novel is prolonged and complex, pitting the heritage of the West against the emerging historical consciousness of traditionally oppressed people, and specifically of black Americans and Africans, whose contemporary task is to discover how they fit into an alien framework.

As the title of the novel suggests, Max Reddick is representative man. At the deepest level, he is both historical man and existential man. His professional success and mobility are simply masks obscuring a reality that Franz Fanon illuminated in *The Wretched of the Earth*—that genocide, caused by the imperialistic imperative, can occur in subtle and ingenious ways. Refining his own historical consciousness in the course of his life, Max Reddick discovers that he has been disinherited and that he has no true country. His cry is an existential acknowledgment of his predicament, and also an assertion of self in face of biological and political death.

Aware of the immediacy of biological death, he tries to cling
to the beauties of the world. Thinking of his Dutch ex-wife,
he dreams of canals: "Now they would be reflecting with
aching clarity the marvelous painter's sky. The barges and
boats would be on the way in, and soon the ducks and swans
would be tucking their necks in to sleep. He had to sleep
soon, too; it might prolong his life."[5] He gradually develops
an awareness of historical death, and thus his cry is of a different order; it is the cry of a man who refuses to be peripheral to the course of history, who will not go quietly to
the grave. In both aspects of his persona, Reddick moves
from understanding to action. He resists, he rebels, and he
dies. A modern Meursault, he learns finally that the cry of the
rebel is the only dignified cry in a hopelessly absurd world.

Williams's treatment of history through fiction, with
broad historical currents influencing the lives of all characters in *The Man Who Cried I Am*, has traditional elements. In
scope and stylistic method he appears close to nineteenth-
century writers of historical fiction like Thackeray and
Tolstoy. Essentially, Williams has always been a realist in fiction—a debt that he would acknowledge in his homage to
Millet in *Mothersill and the Foxes.* He has been loathe to
abandon the realist's craft for the vagaries of contemporary
fiction, and he believes that fiction should be able to
transmit values to a broad reading public. Thus there are
always "popular" elements in his novels. *The Man Who
Cried I Am* reads at a superficial level like a picaresque
novel, with Reddick moving through a rich fictive universe
populated by artists, politicians, and available women; at a
similar level it also owes something to the standard structures of detective fiction. As vehicles designed to appeal to a
popular audience, they serve a function, but they also are integral to Williams's creation of highly dramatized lives linked
to a continuous historical landscape.

As with most nineteenth-century writers of this genre,
Williams is also willing to give some twists to history in
order, as Herbert Butterfield once observed, to subdue it to
the demands of the novel. Some of the wrenches are relatively
simple, while others necessarily involve him in revisionist in-
terpretations and in political prophecies. One basic but

highly effective device that he uses in *The Man Who Cried I Am* is to create personas for easily identifiable contemporary figures. The most sustained application of this technique, and the most successful, is the depiction of Harry Ames, an exceedingly vivid figure and the fictive embodiment of Richard Wright.[6] Other significant personas include Paul Durrell as Martin Luther King, Jr.; Minister Q, treated far more sympathetically than Durrell,[7] as Malcolm X; Marion Dawes as James Baldwin; and the unnamed president for whom Reddick briefly works as John Kennedy. These translucent covers might tantalize some readers, a gambit common to much popular fiction today, but Williams had a more serious intention in mind. Basically, this technique distances fictional characters from actual historical figures—just enough so that we understand that Williams wants us to judge his novel as a work of art, not as a form of documentary. His avatars convey a sense of history and of the historical figures they are modeled upon without detracting unduly from the persistent focus on Max Reddick, who is a fairly good cover himself for Williams and for Chester Himes.[8] Unlike Dos Passos's method in *U.S.A.*, Williams never permits history and its figures to usurp his fictive universe. Reddick is almost pure central consciousness in the novel (there are very few shifts—perhaps there should have been none—to less restricted points of view), and we apprehend history through his eyes, as it functions as a deterministic force, a tragic cycle or, as Williams terms it, a "vicious cycle" (9) that haunts the central character throughout the novel.

The Artist as Rebel

The metaphor of the circle, or the cycle repeating itself, informs *The Man Who Cried I Am*. Williams, who in the novel perceives history and personality as cyclical phenomena, casts himself in terms of tone as a cynical Spenglerian—an artist with a tragic view of history. Events in the novel return inevitably to an evil source. Action opens and closes in Amsterdam, an ideal setting, for it was Dutch traders who introduced slavery to America. Reddick ponders this historical fact at the start of the novel: " '*A Dutch man o'warre that sold us twenty negars,'* John Rolfe wrote, *Well, you-all, I bring myself. Free! Three hundred and forty-five years after Jamestown. Now . . . how's that for the circle come full?"* (4). Max, enjoying an ironic reversal, does not perceive at the outset of his last day that deeper historical ironies still keep him running in the same captive circle, from New York, to Europe, to Africa, and back. He knows a lot, but he must shed his boredom before he can emerge as a rebel: "He was bored with New Deals and Square Deals and New Frontiers and Great Societies; suspicious of the future, mistrusting of the past. He was sure of one thing: that he was; that he existed. The pain in the ass told him so"(18).

Max's "pain in the ass," functioning literally and symbolically,[9] had bothered him since the late 1930s, but it is only in the final stages of cancer that he begins to consider the background of his condition. His entire career as reporter and as a literary artist trained to see things close up prepares him for the final perception that he is suffering from a terminal historical sickness. In fact, integrity as an artist— despite the fierce assaults waged on him by the parasites and cannibals of the literary establishment, which Williams depicts brilliantly in the novel—permits Reddick to survive to a point where he can make final revelations about himself and his identity. Close in personal relationships to only a few people (to Margrit; to Lillian Patch, an earlier fiancee who had died after an abortion; to Harry Ames; to the literary critic, Bernard Zutkin; and to Minister Q), Max evolves better as an artist. He sifts the modern landscape, reports and interprets events, measures public figures, and determines continental drifts. As an artist, he is the custodian of history and of public truths.

The role of the artist is a theme already treated in Williams's earlier fiction, but in *The Man Who Cried I Am*, the author is interested in the idea of the artist as the curator of social, political, and historical reality. There are false artists, people like Alphonse Edwards and Roger Wilkinson, black expatriates who, functioning as CIA operatives, liquidate Max at the end of the novel. There are "great ones" like Burke McGalpin, the alcoholic incarnation of William Faulkner. There are the hucksters and manipulators who form the artistic establishment. In minority, there are artists who are rebels, people like Harry Ames, from whom Max takes lessons throughout the book. Without Ames, Max might have remained an artist who knew how "to scheme and jive, dance in the sandbox, Tom, kiss behinds" (46). He does learn to make his way as a professional writer, but he apprehends a larger task as an artist—to explore the ambiguities and obscure horrors of the world. His task, and his burden, is to function as a Melville, "a super Confidence Man, a Benito Cereno saddened beyond death" (209).

In this role, Max Reddick must see through reality to terrifying truths at the core of the universe. The world and its history are for Max a white whale, fierce and seemingly inscrutable, yet offering secrets for those who can plumb the depths. The supreme artist must be able to expose the absurd, demonic, and malignant forces that govern the world. As a young reporter for the New York *Democrat*, Max covers and becomes obsessed with the case of Moses Boatwright, a black Harvard graduate who had killed a white man and eaten his heart and genitals. Perhaps the most powerfully conceived and written episode in the novel, this scene serves as a paradigm of humanity forced to recognize its ludicrous and terrifying condition. The Boatwright case becomes an obsession for Reddick because of the extreme commentary on racial relationships that it presents. Described as a grotesque creature, as a spiderlike insect with "eyes like two searchlights in need of cleaning" (57), Boatwright, with a master's degree in philosophy, was "born seeing precisely" (58). Madman, victim, executioner, pervert, philospher, and prophet, he tells Reddick: "This world is an illusion, Mr. Reddick, but it can be real. I went prowling on the jungle side of the road where few people ever go because there are things there, crawling, slimy, terrible things that always remind us that down deep we are rotten, stinking beasts" (58–59). Boatwright is a detestable yet unsettling figure for Reddick, a person functioning as a harrowing, ritualistic commentary on human development. He is historical man reduced to cannibalism. He haunts the novel, is a grim presence at its conclusion as Reddick learns the final cannibalistic irony: "The coming of age, Negro set at Negro in the name of God and Country. Or was it the ultimate trap?" (401).

Max's entire career as an artist and his pilgrimage as a man

is a "coming of age." After the publication of Reddick's first
novel, he is told by Harry Ames: "I'm the way I am, the kind
of writer I am, and you may be too, because I'm a black man;
therefore, we're in rebellion; we've got to be. We have no
other function as valid as that one" (49). Ames, as literary
father to Reddick and to other black writers, moves into expatriation with his white wife, Charlotte, following an incident based on that critical event in Williams's own life, retraction of his fellowship by the American Academy in Rome.
That Williams chose to place a key autobiographical event
into the novel through Ames rather than through Reddick
suggests the author's degrees of identification with his two
main male characters. Ames, older, wiser, more consistently
militant, and finally more cynical than his protege, toughens
the political tone of *The Man Who Cried I Am*. Appearing intermittently in the book, Ames is Williams's most vividly
realized character. A doppelgänger in many ways, he is what
Max Reddick will become.

Williams's treatment of Reddick is more complex and ambitious than his sharp portraiture of Ames. His intention with
Reddick is twofold: to create him as a relatively individualized
character, a strategy employed in Part 1 (the longest of the
four major sections, consisting of twelve chapters); and to
establish him finally as a generalized historical type.[10] His
mission as an artist coincides with his historical destiny. His
constant rectal itch—symbolic of a world literally eating at
him—determines his role as an artist: "It was all eating at
Max now. . . . He found himself wanting to get away and
write. He wanted to do with the novel what Charlie Parker
was doing to music—tearing it up and remaking it; basing it
on nasty, nasty blues and overlaying it with the deep overriding tragedy not of Dostoevsky, but an American who
knew of the consequences to come" (209). (The American
alluded to is Melville.[11]) Yet there is a disparity between
what Max wants to do as an artist and what he actually ac-
complishes. Until he receives the King Alfred Plan, he remains, in Harry Ames's description of him, somewhat "anal,"
a fact about himself that he is only too well aware of, as
when, in accepting a job at *Pace*, he asks himself, "whose ass
was he kissing?" (223). Writing and publishing "Negro"

novels, moving successfully through the journalistic jungle, advising the president, Reddick has a tendency to lose sight of his essential self. This tendency is never acute, for he is a shrewd and perceptive observer of the world he lives in. Moreover, he is kept in touch with his racial and historical identity by his subconscious alter ego, Saminone ("Sambo-in-one-person"), with whom he conducts discourses during moments of drug-induced revery. Doing the dozens—engaging in a ritualistic game of verbal insults—with Saminone,[12] Reddick is forced to acknowledge a certain existential pride:

> *How does a man trap himself so completely?*
>
> *Is you askin'?*
>
> *Yes, I'm asking.*
>
> *Pride, pride, turrible pride.*
>
> *You've got to do better than that.*
>
> *Oh, no I don't. You so goddamn busy tryin' t' prove you am.*
>
> *You were talking about pride.*
>
> *The same thing, burr-head, the same goddamn thing.*
>
> *Hee, haw . . . . (295)*

Max asserts a personal "I" throughout the novel, but tends to subdue the role of artist as rebel—the necessary role of the man and artist in full comprehension of the historical and political roots of oppression. Reddick's role as rebel, which constitutes his true assertion of self, comes only during the last day of his life. Transcribing the contents of the King Alfred Plan to Minister Q by long distance phone, he acts decisively to expose the terrors of modern history, even as he assures the doom of Minister Q and himself.

The King Alfred Plan activates Max's latent cynicism, his tragic understanding of history; it is the corroboration of lessons learned over three decades on three continents. The Plan is the inevitable outcome in a pattern of historical determinism that spans centuries. In his last letter to Max, which accompanies the Plan, Harry Ames had written, "How goddamn different this world would have been if there had been no Charles Martel in Tours in 732!" (222)—an allusion to the high point in the Moorish conquests. Instead of a dark-

skinned victory, the Western World was to witness white
ascendancy over subsequent centuries. Whether in America,
Europe, or Africa, Max is haunted by "faces out of nightmares," as Bernard Zutkin terms them, by a civilization
capable of genocide. Used consistently by the author as a
vehicle for exploring the violent and oppressive configura-
tions of history, Max Reddick emerges as a rebel fighting
history itself. That he is defeated is not an immaterial fact.
Nevertheless, in finding death through rebellion, Max
achieves a fully integrated sense of self; the tragic historical
philosophy finally forced upon him by the King Alfred Plan
permits him a last revolutionary act.

The Embodiment of History

In keeping with Lukács's dictum that protagonists in
historical fiction should serve as representatives of broad
historical currents, that "their psychology and destiny
always represent social trends and historical forces," [13] John
Williams succeeds in creating a central figure whose entire
consciousness and behavior are the embodiment of history.
"Caught up in the spin of history" (223), Max Reddick
knows that his racial and cultural identity has been disfig-
ured and destroyed: "What they wouldn't do, the white
folks, to keep you from having a history, the better, after all,
to protect theirs" (223). Thus the King Alfred Plan is only one
form of genocide. Far more insidious is the form of cultural
genocide that deprives people of their history, and consequently of their identity. History, manipulated and written
by Western powers, is a vast conspiracy that feeds on the
corpses of millions. It is a universal horror that makes the
isolated act of a Moses Boatwright, or the planned execu-
tions of Max and Minister Q, merely emblematic. Meditating
on the terrors of history, Max feels that history turns on a
basic question, How many men can I kill? "No, Moses, your
little horror was no match for Hiroshima and history; no
match for human lampshades, Zyklon B, cakes of soap made
from human fats" (68). Reddick has been witness to contemporary horrors—to fascism in Spain, to the nine million killed
in Europe, to the war in Angola. He concludes that certain

peoples are condemned by history, that they are programmed to be destroyed by it. Thinking again of Moses Boatwright toward the end of the novel, after he has read all the documents relating to the King Alfred Plan, he admits a philosophical affinity: "Man is nature, nature man, and all crude and raw, stinking, vicious, evil . . . . It is still eat, drink and be murderous, for tomorrow I may be among the murdered" (377).

Within the grim historical universe that John Williams plots in *The Man Who Cried I Am*, any affirmation must be painful and provisional. Max Reddick, carrying with him the sickly odor of putrefaction in one of the most chilling patterns of imagery in the novel, retains the will to resist, and this is affirmation in itself. Despite all the sharply noted details of his adult life—his struggle for success and acceptance, his tribulations as an artist, his loves and lusts, his yearnings for a simple, natural life in a world that can be infinitely beautiful—he remains with readers as a mythic figure. He is a version of contemporary historical allegory, the embodiment of a series of ideas (as are Kafka's K., Camus's Meursault, and Sartre's Rocquentin) that map the human condition in the twentieth century. At a time when concentration camps still existed in the United States,[14] Williams offers a hero who rebels against them. Resistance to evil is necessary, suggests Williams, before life can be good.

Writing in 1964, as *The Man Who Cried I Am* was starting to take shape, Williams observed, "Novelists would do well to remember that when the works of the scholar-historians create doubt in the researcher's mind, the researcher then turns to literature as a primary source for confirmation or correction. If the truth of a time, a people, a state is not available anywhere else, let it be in the novel."[15] *The Man Who Cried I Am* conveys historical interpretation. In the novel, which is one of the most ambitious works by an American writer in the 1960s, Williams asks us to recognize the haunting historical continuity of past, present, and future. He provides us with facts and with prophecies and tests our understanding of fiction and reality. He paints a vast canvas that depicts lives caught in a historical labyrinth. At the same time, he urges resistance to seemingly inexorable forces, even if resistance and rebellion mean death. For

Williams, writing out of the multiple traumas of the decade, history and politics had become the organic stuff of fiction. The prophetic insights in *The Man Who Cried I Am* would cast shadows over the darkening world that Williams was to treat in his next two novels.

Chapter Five
Apocalypse: *Sons of Darkness, Sons of Light*

John Williams's fifth novel, *Sons of Darkness, Sons of Light*, was published in 1969. Calling it "a novel of some probability," he moved away from the structural complexities of *Sissie* and *The Man Who Cried I Am* to simpler narrative devices, using the techniques of popular fiction to advance a fundamentally unidealistic prospect of American race relations. *Sons of Darkness, Sons of Light* is both a retrospective on the decade and a forecast of the future. With its action set in 1973, the novel contains the author's bleakest vision of the American future, an apocalyptic projection of race warfare and urban conflagration. In certain ways a topical novel, lacking the formal depth or thoughtfulness of his previous two novels, *Sons of Darkness, Sons of Light* nevertheless reveals a writer moving beyond earlier fictive statements, even as the book capitalizes on the events of the period.

Williams did not spend a great deal of time writing this novel, and occasionally he has taken an unnecessarily dim view of it:

Sons of Darkness, Sons of Light in many ways was a pot boiler for me anyhow. I sat down and wrote it comparatively quickly compared to the other books. This was a reaction to my continued poverty after *The Man Who Cried I Am* came along. It looked as if finally, I'd be able to make a little money and help both boys who were in college at that time. The critical acclaim was good, but I was just as poor as I had always been. And as a matter of fact, that book in paperback is all over the place, but the paperback pub-

lisher tells me it hasn't made a dime. The whole thing is so damn
crazy it's better not to go into it. So, I sat down and wrote this
book. I think it's one of my worst novels. It brought in more paperback money than *The Man Who Cried I Am*. And it's just the way
things happen in America.[1]

Although a potboiler, or what Williams has termed an "A to
Z" book, *Sons of Darkness, Sons of Light* reflects the
author's vision of a turbulent decade. Behind him was a
litany of assasinations, murders, and disruptions: the death
of Medgar Evers; the killing of the four black girls in the
bombing of their Sunday school in Birmingham on
September 15, 1953; the murders of John F. Kennedy,
Robert Kennedy, Malcolm X, and Martin Luther King, Jr.;
and the death of Viola Liuzzo (a figure alluded to in the
novel). Also noted by Williams were the limited successes of
the CORE Freedom Riders; of nonviolent resistance; of
demonstrations like the march on Washington for civil rights
in which Williams had participated on August 28, 1963.
Finally, as immediate legacies and ones important to the
novel, were the urban riots of the period. *Sons of Darkness,
Sons of Light* assumes as its setting a futuristic landscape that
is the logical continuation of the disruptions of the decade.
In the immediate past of this futuristic novel are the spon-
taneous riots of 1964 in Harlem, Bedford-Stuyvesant,
Rochester, Jersey City, and Philadelphia; the seven-day riot
in Watts in August of 1965; and the ghetto rioting in 125
cities that followed the assassination of Martin Luther King,
Jr. Looking toward a new decade, Williams actually sensed
more possibility than probability for a continuation of national violence. Setting his new novel in the so-called long
hot summer of 1973, he provides an extension of the
catastrophic element that had been inherent in the history of
the 1960s and also in *The Man Who Cried I Am*.
    The central figure in this political "entertainment" (which
is closer in spirit to the fiction of Graham Greene than to the
slick presentations of political despair by writers like Len
Deighton and John Le Carré) is Eugene Browning. A former
college professor of political science who has left the profession in order to engage in direct political activity as second-
in-command at New York's Institute for Racial Justice, Gene

Browning is in a sense the resurrection of Max Reddick. Like Reddick he is coolly intellectual, a professional in touch with current events. Browning is essentially a rebel, however, the revolutionary that Max Reddick became only in the last hours of his life. Although his sense of justice is rooted more in Old Testament strictures than in any sophisticated contemporary ideology, Browning adheres to the existentialist injunction that authentic behavior depends on proper understanding of the situation and the ability to act on the basis of that understanding. That he does not suffer excessively for his political action, or even assume the burden of history, indicates the limitations that Williams has placed on character and action in the novel. Williams has not attempted to duplicate here the same political and historical density that had been the hallmark of his previous novel. But the work is political fiction nevertheless. Browning is an engaging figure who, through the author's shifting point of view, must share the stage with a number of other representatives of various political persuasions. His actions actually precipitate urban holocausts from New York to Los Angeles. Yet like a figure in a futuristic fairy tale, he is able to walk away from the destruction that he has spawned.

Political Fantasy

Fairy tales, of course, are ultimately very serious forms of fiction. They are rooted in myth and project dark truths reaching to the center of human consciousness. They illuminate the nature of evil in the world. They are "fantasy" of very high probability. *Sons of Darkness, Sons of Light*, constructed as political fantasy, also engages the reader at a mythic level. Here there is literally a contest between the forces of darkness and the forces of light, with the forces of light tending to be either amoral or decidedly ambiguous in their actions. When Browning, whose name prefigures the clearer symbolism that Williams would employ for the protagonist in his next book, *Captain Blackman*, learns at the start of the novel that a white policeman, Corrigan, has killed an unarmed black youth, he decides to seek revenge by paying for a contract to have the cop assassinated. Williams, who does not provide any serious motivational background

for this critical decision, thus introduces Browning in the
mold of a popular hero in quest of justice.

As political hero, Browning is an avenging angel cast upon
a violent historical stage. Awakening in chapter 1 on "the
day" when he sets his plan in motion, he speculates on a
drawbridge in a painting by Van Gogh and on the course of
history:

He had once met a couple who told of driving around Arles in
search of the drawbridge, only to discover that it had been
destroyed in 1935 because it was so old. Nineteen thirty-five was
Ethiopia, was China, and there had been 1936 and Spain. A
political scientist, like a historian, had an ear for dates, dates when
great mistakes had been made, the ones you snapped your fingers
over when they were charted out and found to be true moments
when history could have changed; true forks in true roads.[2]

Coming between the careful assessment of the relationship
between character and history in *The Man Who Cried I Am*
and the remarkable archetypal presentation of documentary
history in *Captain Blackman*, this orchestration of history
and personality is too transparent. Williams does not examine history or character closely in *Sons of Darkness, Sons
of Light*. Instead, within the confines of popular fiction, he
deals with surface impressions, broad action, and intriguing
prophecies. Browning is a protagonist who believes he can
change history through a single application of violence. He
wants a "good world," one better than the closed, hot urban
universe surrounding him. But against the twin enemies of
"political power and big business" (10) he can only locate
violent alternatives.

Just as Browning discards peaceful solutions to racial problems, he recognizes that his dream of middle-class security
and respectability has been illusory. For one thing, he is
overwhelmed by vocational anxiety. As a political science
professor, he had not questioned sufficiently the nature of
the American political system or traditional education in the
United States, and the general failings in the social structure.
Two years in New York at the IRJ has placed him at the
center of the movement, but again he is harried and unful-
filled. Moreover, the urban and political battlefields in which

he operates are reinforced by domestic tension. His wife, Val, to whom he has been married for twenty years, is chic and beautiful, but sullen and resentful. She dislikes New York and Browning's job, and has an aversion to the white boy whom her older daughter, Nora, is dating. Chris, the younger daughter, is flip and resilient, the only survivor in the family who can shed the tensions that are consuming everyone else. The dreams that have so much thematic importance in the fiction of John Williams are absent at the start of *Sons of Darkness, Sons of Light*. In this novel, readers sense the failure of the American dream, and an alternate vision of a world lurching toward racial nightmare.

Beginning with the assumption that America is a fundamentally violent nation, Williams presents a catalog of people who contend with or perpetrate it. Basically, there is a triad of individuals who subscribe to retributive violence: Browning himself; the aging Mafia don who arranges for the liquidation of Corrigan; and Itzhak Hod, the professional international freedom fighter who assassinates Corrigan and who, at a more deftly human and comic level is (like a character out of the short fiction of Bernard Malamud) a middle-aged Jew in search of a child bride. Browning is a man who is tired of discussing the system from behind a professor's lectern or an administrator's desk. Separated by his professional training from the people in the streets, he believes his task is to initiate a symbolic act that will partially relieve injustice and oppression, and also transmit a symbolic message to the power structure that black resistance has entered a new phase, one in which no black life can be taken with impunity. Browning elects to identify himself with the struggle, even as he attempts to remove himself from retribution by having the Mafia carry out the contract.

Browning succeeds within the carefully circumscribed arena of retributive violence that he maps. His plan to have Corrigan killed succeeds, and he escapes the consequences of his act. Williams clearly wants us to sympathize with Browning's reluctance to accept responsibility for anything beyond the murder itself, as well as with his desire to escape detection—to adopt a politically and personally circumspect or secretive attitude toward the act. To the extent that there is an amoral universe in *Sons of Darkness, Sons of Light* and a certain abstraction of violence and character, Williams enlists reader sympathies for individuals who commit murders and who hasten the world toward destruction.

Essentially, Williams plays with political positions and existential attitudes through Browning and other characters in the novel. His fictive world, half-way between contemporary American realities and futuristic prophecies, cannot bear close ethical scrutiny. Browning's decision to have a cop killed throws the United States into chaos, hurling it toward a shattering endpoint that can only result in the destruction of cities and racial genocide, and these conclusions radiate beyond the actual end of the novel. Browning, who helps to create this world, and who should assume complicity for it, escapes such ethical judgment. Instead he is projected as a new sort of existentialist who does not have to suffer or assume responsibility for his acts. On this matter Williams has observed:

Now, one of the reasons why, I suppose, I did that Browning thing was to somehow tell people that it doesn't matter how much education you've got if you're black. There's no such thing as removing one's self from it. You're always to some degree involved. And as Sartre, a Johnny-come-lately, has just said recently, the intellectual has got to put his body on the line as well as his mind. Now he says that knowing full well that many people are not about to do so. But, if you're talking about young intellectuals who are probably not that well known in France, that's a different matter. They can get hurt. They can be killed. So, the question of putting one's body on the line with one's mind becomes something you might want to equivocate about. And that's exactly Browning's position.[3]

In a sense readers are also left to equivocate about their reaction to Browning's political behavior. Yet if all acts have their political consequences, then Browning clearly tries to avoid this causal relationship, seeking instead his own separate peace at the start of the holocaust.

The second figure in the novel who endorses retributive violence is Don Mantini. Retired and in his seventies, Mantini is a loving Godfather, somewhat in the mold of Puzo's Don

Corleone. From his West Side penthouse that overlooks Central Park, the Don surveys a world that seems to be sadly lacking in traditional values. Fascinated by Browning's plan, which he has learned about through a nephew whom Browning knows (Williams makes coincidental plotting work very well in the novel), the Don is eager to meet this schemer whose sense of fundamental justice matches the Don's own sense of Sicilian justice. The Don, representing in all likelihood a nonexistent philosophical-romantic branch of the Mafia that seems to be the unique invention of American writers, perceives the world as a battleground and society as being ruled by power structures predicated on oppression and exploitation. He has an instinctive mistrust of the forces of institutionalized education, knowing that "books did not help many people born on Sicilian soil . . . that while the men in the cafe might have grudging respect for books, they feared them because those who knew books had always oppressed them" (38). An apostle of intuitive wisdom rather than desiccated book knowledge, the Don likes Browning because he is committed to a cause, because he contracts for a killing not out of selfish or vengeful motives but for a higher goal.

Although Browning has an initial aversion to the immaculately dressed old man who takes an interest in him, he understands the mutuality of their positions; their place in the American scheme of things; their collective destiny in the melting pot. Over dinner on a hot August night, they discuss the relationship between intelligence and violence, and between capitalism, politics, and power. The Don, likening politics to an octopus, tells Browning things that it had taken the college professor years of formal education to discover. Separation from the mainstream makes it imperative, as Browning has discovered, that they be "as tough as the next guy or tougher" (192) in order to survive in a hostile environment.

Itzhak Hod, the gun for hire, shares the sense of history subscribed to by Browning and Don Mantini. Recently arrived in America, Hod is the traditional Jew, the new immigrant, the comic assassin, and the middle-aged lover—all in one. A Polish Jew who has fought and killed anti-Semites, Fascists,

Nazis, Arabs, and an assortment of political victims all his
life, Hod is a killer with a heart and soul. He is an interna-
tionalist who carries with him more vividly than Browning
and the Don the horrors of the twentieth century. Hod is the
philosopher of death, the connoisseur of killing. "You killed
for money, as he had been doing, which was better than
doing it because you liked it, but not nearly as honest as killing in a rage as he had long ago. Or you killed for country.
And that could involve killing for all the other reasons"
(144–45). Hod kills Corrigan without even knowing that he
is a cop, but after learning his victim's identity, he becomes
preoccupied with racial history in America to the point
that—as a gift to the nation—he determines to liquidate a
Southerner, Herman Mahler, who had killed three black
coeds and gone free. Finding himself hiding in a closet of
Mahler's house with a black militant, Trotman, whose sister
had been one of the slain coeds, Hod instructs the young
revolutionary in the proper killing of the victim with a
silencer. Operating in the same magic circle of violence as
Browning and Mantini, Hod escapes detection and returns to
New York to marry Mickey, a twenty-one-year-old Jewish
girl. Together they fly immediately to Israel where they will
begin a new life in a rugged settlement. Hod is present in the
novel as a benign assassin of people who apparently deserve
to be killed and also as a comic figure who deserves love and
peace in his life. He is a "son of light" who both informs and
modulates the darker impulses in the novel. Just as Hod gets
his bride, Don Mantini escapes across New York's bridges
just before they are blown up, and goes fishing. Browning,
for his part, makes love at a retreat on Long Island's south
fork. The comic-pastoral rhythms defining these three characters' lives strengthen Williams's intention to keep the
novel balanced between the apocalyptic-futuristic tones
determined by political action and the lighter tones that can
be preserved residually in private lives.

Black Power

Browning, Mantini and Hod—the triumverate whose conspiracy precipitates the cataclysm in the novel—are juxtaposed against a larger number of individuals whom

Williams creates as a cross section of black power in the United States. In his capacity as fund raiser for the IRJ, Browning travels the continent, learning how black economic and political power is co-opted, assimilated, or neutralized by the broader white power structure. Williams projects a critical and occasionally cynical tone in his depiction of the varieties of black power in America as represented by set characters. Bill Barton, the head of IRJ, an organization that seems in part to be patterned after the NAACP, is an opportunist who is willing to betray black revolutionaries in exchange for government funding. He is a fictional prefiguration of the devastating portrait of Martin Luther King, Jr., that Williams would erect in *The King God Didn't Save*. Linked to the IRJ as main sources of funding are the nation's black millionaires whom Williams satirizes. The "cream of black business" survives by virtue of its accommodation to the larger white business community and is often baldly exploitative of the black community. These businessmen, allied to activists like Barton who work within the system, control the middle and right of the black political spectrum, leaving the left to radicals and revolutionaries whose methods and attitudes represent scarce improvement in terms of solving America's problems.

Williams sympathizes more with the black radicals and revolutionaries who appear in the novel than with those who operate within the system. Nevertheless, he does expose their limited abilities to transform American society, as well as the sham and deception of which they are capable. Dr. Millard Jessup, a young Los Angeles professional, plays at revolution with his wealth, erecting guerrilla camps and staging areas deep in the California mountains from which the black revolution will be launched. Jessup, however, has entered into an unholy alliance with the John Birch Society, an alliance that Williams thinks is a suicidally false strategy. Purer in their revolutionary intentions are the young radicals Morris Greene and Leonard Trotman, whose plan for urban war and the destruction of New York's bridges and tunnels on Labor Day is linked to a concrete set of demands on the American government. Yet even they lack the human element of mutual trust on which the revolution must be predicated. Greene, suspicious of Trotman's admittedly implausible account of the Birmingham episode involving Hod, locks Trotman in a closet over the Labor Day weekend. The act conveys the knowledge to both that there is nothing special about their revolution, that it contains the same seeds of corruption and self-destruction that has accompanied most revolutions in the past. Betrayal, Williams infers, is built into black politics in America.

Speaking about the radical black politics of the period, Williams observed:

In the first place—it may be a black thing, I don't know—we seem to abhor secrecy. You can't have a militant black group in this country unless it's infiltrated. It's just impossible. The only groups you can have that are valid and functioning and haven't done anything yet are those that operated in total secrecy. We just don't seem to be able to pull that off. I think that's what's totally necessary in this society that is shot through with surveillance systems, peoples, codes, and so forth.[4]

Williams was skeptical about the ability of black militant organizations to succeed in the United States. In *Sons of Darkness, Sons of Light* he exposes the human failings of black revolutionaries. Nevertheless, they do succeed in creating a national urban revolution, although long-range outcomes are unknown.

On a national scale, the revolution assuredly is not coordinated, but rather a chain reaction of localized responses to Browning's "little act of violence" (82). Williams depicts the escalating violence during his long hot summer with considerable narrative skill, oscillating from white to black urban retaliation on a broadening scale of intensity. When white youths invade the black sections of fifty cities and the police orchestrate Operation Black Out in response to cop killings, the black communities respond with organized violence. Williams depicts the resistance of black communities to organized white violence with a narrative zest bordering on the comic:

Old men and old women, children, youths, adults of middle age. Zip guns, rifles, shotguns, automatics, revolvers. Lye rained down along with pots, pans, pieces of furniture, dishes, glasses, lengths of iron, lead and zinc pipe; bricks from tottering chimneys, pots of boiling hot water, pans of cold water, knives, ice picks, broken lamps; more than one number-10 cast iron skillet slung down from the darkened windows and into the milling cops. The Negroes fought in silence too this time, and they shot out as many streetlights as the cops who were trying to return fire. The police shot blindly upwards at the shapes of buildings. (234)

Comedy prevails over the vision of chaos that Williams projects in this instance. In fact, Williams has a penchant for comedy, satire, and ironic moral inversions in *Sons of Darkness, Sons of Light*, and this makes for complex tonalities in the novel.

An Intellectual Experiment

By exploiting the devices of popular and utopian fiction, Williams was able to present some of the most urgent problems facing America in the 1960s in a provocative but nevertheless emotionally detached manner. The urban upheaval that he develops in the novel does not possess deep resonances of horror. Instead, it seems to be presented as an intellectual exercise as well as a fictive puzzle that the intrigued reader must follow from one episode of suspense to another. Essentially, Williams in *Sons of Darkness, Sons of Light* hit on new ways to express the analytical and declarative impulse so evident in his earlier fiction. As a form of dystopian prophecy, the novel does not predict categorically that racial warfare is inevitable. Williams assumes that such conflict has always existed, that given the condition of the times in the 1960s it could become endemic in the cities of America. But on a much broader level of meaning, the novel is about the consequences of injustice, the forms of violence—both reactionary and revolutionary—created by an unjust society, and the strategies available to people who believe in the possibility of a better world.

Although *Sons of Darkness, Sons of Light* is not a better novel than *The Man Who Cried I Am*, it does represent a significant advance by the author between his fourth and fifth novels. The earlier work is largely unrelieved by any degree of conviction on Williams's part that the power struc-

ture can be altered. On the other hand, *Sons of Darkness,
Sons of Light* depicts a revolutionary situation and a world
where people fight oppression with everything from explo-
sives strong enough to destroy bridges to pots and pans.
Williams transcribes into individual and mass revolution the
incipiently revolutionary acts that Max Reddick attempted
fruitlessly at the end of his life. Even as he implies that the
tactics of revolutionaries are limited, fragile, and perhaps
doomed to ultimate failure, the author seems to exult in the
ability of a single man like Browning, and urban minorities,
to make the American landscape shudder. In short, he invokes a cardinal axiom expressed by Franz Fanon in *The
Wretched of the Earth*. As Noel Schraufnagel has noted of the
novel: "It illustrates a theory propounded by Franz Fanon
which suggests that violence tends to unify an oppressed
people. From an individual point of view, it acts as a cleans-
ing force which frees a person from his despair at watching
the world go by without doing anything to stop the oppressive forces that work against him. Violence in the face of
oppression restores self-respect."[5] Carefully planned revolutionary acts are emblems of resistance and solidarity, not
necessarily final solutions to imperial power.

Browning is not so much the pure revolutionary as the
metaphysical rebel. He assumes responsibility for the
millions of people who have worked hard all their lives for a
slice of the American dream, and he understands the ironic
reversals that have attended his sole rebellious act: "The simple, selective violent act, calculated to deliver a message, had
become magnified. All the black populace he had been trying
to save from slaughter looked like it was being slaughtered
after all" (269). He is humanized to the extent that he is confused by moral ambiguities and natural failings, even as he
pursues his act of rebellion with single-minded purpose.
Retreating to Sag Harbor at the end of the novel to rejoin his
family, Browning resolves to extricate himself from IRJ and
to return to teaching, but as a revisionist professor who will
"teach down the system." Discovering that his wife has been
having an affair, he sympathizes with the desperation that
people feel about their lives, and he forgives her. Joined by
Woody, Nora's boyfriend who arrives with weapons, Gene

Browning senses a solidarity that will hold against the imminent violence that surrounds them and the nation.

Finally, Williams succeeds in harnessing seemingly disparate impulses in *Sons of Darkness, Sons of Light*—the bloody vision of civil war and urban destruction; and the utopian promise inherent in such virtues as friendship, love, charity, trust, and altruistic action. There is in the novel a strong light, not a normal moral light but an Old Testament light, that illuminates the pages of the novel. The people who outlast the holocaust, all tested by violence and by death, seem to be a new brand of American survivors, people who can inform beneficially the future of America. The Don, along with his nephew Peter and his faithful companion Carlo, retreats into the New England backwoods to fish, seeking the clean breast of the new world all over again. Itzhak Hod and his child bride embark on a voyage literally to build a new world, a microcosmic community of patriots for a nation. Browning and his wife, rebuilding their marriage, learn again "the way of things." Woody and Nora, shedding the racial phobias of an older America, embody the promise of interracial harmony. Val, observing that "It sounds like the end of the world" (273), does not possess the double perspective that Williams has built into the novel, but she does provide in her statement a gloss on the main thematic duality: The world in certain ways is coming to an end, but well-intentioned people will remain to rebuild it.

In *Sons of Darkness, Sons of Light*, John Williams uses the modes of popular fiction—anarchic fantasy, crime and mystery, espionage—to fashion an absorbing narrative of doom. Action moves rapidly through sequential chapters that shift focus in scene, episode, and character in order to sustain suspense. The author persistently examines various forms of American violence and such alternatives to it as resistance and revolution. The result is an exciting novel, designed to stir readers at an almost visceral level of response, but intriguing in its intellectual contours. The novel is not without its flaws. For example, readers might question the romantic conclusion in which Browning and his wife make love while America burns, a symbolic restorative act perhaps more in keeping with denouements in the pulps than in serious narratives. (When this issue was raised, Williams replied that at the time he wrote the novel, he honestly felt that the only legitimate alternative to the violence of the era was love-making.) Nevertheless, *Sons of Darkness, Sons of Light* is considerably better and more significant than its author might admit. His mild embarrassment over the motives for writing the book should not obscure the fact that it is very well crafted, designed to appeal to a general readership in terms of popular fiction, and successful within this genre. At the same time, it moves beyond the limitations of popular fiction to render an interesting set of propositions about the American future.

In the final analysis, Williams probably could have written an excellent novel of hopelessness if he had eschewed the devices of popular fiction and taken the book more seriously than he did. As it stands, it is an interesting and singular experiment that captures the cross-currents of American political militancy during the period. It offers both political meditation and futuristic speculation, although it is difficult to determine whether or not Williams actually believed in the validity of his prophecies. Like Browning, readers themselves must play the role of political scientists who scrutinize "the whole damned human race" (268) in an effort to understand the way in which every act can have political consequences for the future fate of the nation.

Chapter Six

Dark and Bloody Ground: *Captain Blackman*

History and politics continue to define Williams's fictive world in his sixth novel, *Captain Blackman*, published in May 1972. In this novel, the author takes the American battleground that was inherent in his earlier fiction and gives it both concrete and philosophical embodiment. Using the Vietnam War (a subject that had been absent from his critique of contemporary America) as a historical springboard, Williams presents a panorama of all major wars engaged in by the United States from colonial times to the near future. The most technically complex of his novels and the most daring and original in form, *Captain Blackman* invokes a historically accurate world that is also mythic and timeless. War is an unavoidable historical reality. It is also the symbol of the universal human condition.

The Fiction of War

Major American writers—Crane, Hemingway, Faulkner, Dos Passos, Mailer, and others—have explored American wars to locate both the essence of human behavior and the contours of the national experience. Since 1945, the number of writers concentrating on wars involving the United States has been legion, so much so that American war fiction constitutes a literary mode. Writing in 1954, Malcolm Cowley observed that he had read more than fifty American novels dealing with World Wars I and II, with a disproportionate number centering on the latter.[1] Notable novels have appeared—James Jones's underrated *From Here to Eternity*, Mailer's *The Naked and the Dead*, Cozzens's *Guard of Honor*, Heller's *Catch-22*, Hawkes's *The Cannibal*, and Vonnegut's *Slaughterhouse Five* constitute a significant galaxy of novels dealing with the Second World War.[2] The works mentioned suggest that beyond the primary subject matter common to American war fiction, the forms and structures of the American war novel are varied, ranging from relatively straightforward realism to the literature of involution and the grotesque. What distinguishes John Williams's *Captain Blackman* are the uniqueness of its subject matter, its technical devices, and its structure. *Captain Blackman* is one of the half-dozen or so greatest American war novels, and the most inclusive treatment by any American writer of war and racism in the context of the national experience.

As the title suggests, *Captain Blackman* portrays the experience of the black soldier throughout America's wars. This subject, almost totally neglected in American fiction, had preoccupied Williams for a number of years. His experience in the Navy between 1943 and 1946 had alerted him to institutional racism in the American armed forces, and in the 1950s and 1960s he had made two aborted starts at writing war novels that would have been close to his own personal experiences.[3] The integral role of black combat troops in the Vietnam War, far disproportionate to the percentage of black Americans in the general population, combined with unsettling reports filtering in from bases in the United States and from overseas on the continuing problems of black soldiers, had induced Williams to assemble documentary materials and to petition the Pentagon for permission to travel to Indo-China to conduct original research. Speaking of *Captain Blackman*, Williams observed:

I wanted originally to do it as a nonfictional book, but I kept running into walls. I couldn't raise the magazine money to travel to the places where I wanted to go to get the material. The historical material I had. Wherever I went, I did go to two or three army bases in America, I had those captains and lieutenants hanging on my shoulders. Magazines were not interested in a black man's view of black people in the army. They only wanted the story told by a white guy. A few years ago everybody was talking about this new democracy in the army. This was a white man's interpretation of what was going on. It turns out to have been false. If I had been able to raise the money to do those pieces, the first places I would have gone to would have been the stockades. That's where the truth always is—in the jails. Maybe my reputation preceded me. Not only was I not able to raise the money, but I had difficulty in getting clearance from the Pentagon to make the trip to Vietnam, Thailand, and places like that. So, I decided to do it as a novel just to show that what I wanted to say, I wanted to say badly enough to do it in one form or the other.[4]

Drawing heavily on historical source materials, Williams fashions a rare form of fiction, close to a nonfiction novel yet epic in its narrative proportions. History as narrative and fiction as narrative become mutually reinforcing components in the most radical, both in terms of vision and technique, of Williams's novels.

Captain Abraham Blackman is the fictive embodiment of American military history in general and black military history specifically. Possessing the rectitude of his biblical namesake, Blackman is a huge, towering six-foot four-inch figure—black manhood conceived in heroic proportions. At the start of the novel, pinned in swamp water by Viet Cong AK-478s, Captain Blackman is both in the vanguard of combat—an officer who takes direct responsibility for his troops—and a leader in the black revolution within the army. Contemplating his own death against the almost certain destruction of the men racing to save him, Blackman weighs the price of heroism:

Only yesterday he'd told them again at the end of his black military history seminar that he didn't want any heroes in his company. Things were close to the end, and even if they weren't, they had nothing to prove. He'd told them time and again, these legs with their mushrooming Afros and off-duty dashikis, that they were not the first black soldiers to do what they were doing. He'd gone back to the American Revolution to Prince Estabrook, Peter Salem, Crispus Attucks and all the unnamed rest; from there to the War of 1812, the Civil War, the Plains Wars, the Spanish-American War—all the wars. He'd conducted the seminar during their off-duty time, without the blessing of the brass, with the obvious, smoldering resentment of the Major, who, for some reason, had let him carry on.[5]

Blackman's preoccupations during a moment of physical danger and psychological crisis establish a plausible frame for Williams's complex erection of plot. Deciding to sacrifice himself for his squad, Captain Blackman exposes himself to enemy fire and is hit by multiple rounds of fire. Unconscious, he begins a dream that takes him from the Revolutionary War to the future. Moments of consciousness, set during the rescue and evacuation effort and his period in the hospital, again create the dual time mechanism that Williams had experimented with successfully in *The Man Who Cried I Am*. Ye the historical canvas is much broader in *Captain Blackman*. Refining both his own method and a structuring device that Mark Twain had employed in *A Connecticut Yankee in King Arthur's Court*, Williams combines the realism and the historical factuality of his subject matter with fictive forms that offer the expansiveness of romance. If, as Richard Chase has declared persuasively, the dominant form of American prose fiction is that type of romance tending toward "mythic, allegorical, and symbolistic forms,"[6] then *Captain Blackman*, with its startling range of time and action, of dream and reality, of conscious and unconscious life, can be understood and evaluated only within this tradition.

Williams's powers of descriptive realism in invoking battle scenes are as vivid as any other realistic depictions in conventional war fiction. During his career as an author, however, he constantly has attempted to extend the boundaries of his work. Answering the charge leveled by some critics that *Captain Blackman* was excessively melodramatic, Williams stated in an interview:

There's really no other way to cover so much time and so much real history, and still provide continuity for the reader. My "melodramatic tendencies" arise, I suppose, from my belief that there has to be continuity to the novel. A story must be told. The story must end somewhere near the end of the novel, not on page 60 or 70. So if you draw a horizontal line, you get lots of vertical lines feeding into it which makes the horizontal line grow toward an end where the damn thing should conclude, not somewhere in the middle. I think I work very hard with each book to find the solution of a problem that I'm not always completely aware of. I don't like writing easy books. I don't like writing the same kinds of books stylistically or thematically. So I'm always into new things which I can't always explain.

The horizontal line that Williams speaks of occupies only a few days in Captain Blackman's life. The vertical lines that inform present time in the novel are in a sense the historical foreknowledge that governs Blackman's destiny.

The Novelist and History

As a writer of historical fiction, Williams was increasingly aware of the special integrity such a literary artist must maintain to the craft of a novel and to the presentation of history. "A novelist embarked on a historical work," notes Williams, "becomes a historian in effect, and he must evaluate his character in terms of the time in which his character lived. He is required to be *both* a novelist and a historian."[8] Williams's critique of a book like *The Confessions of Nat Turner* is based precisely on the fact that Styron distorts facts and writes misleading history. The challenge for the true historical novelist is not to distort or reinvent history but to provide a revisionist interpretation of it. This is especially true of black American history. "In America,' writes Williams, "the novelist is only just beginning to correct history. Is it because the losers who have joined their ranks have made them aware of gross manipulation of it or is it because of the losers outside their ranks? In either case, we have viewed history poorly illustrated for too long. The illustrations have been altered, sections have been omitted, and mythographers have filled in the gaps."[9] *Captain Blackman* presents meticulously researched history. At the same time, it relies on remarkable narrative structures that reify and dramatize history for readers whose primary frame of reference remains the novel.

Captain Blackman is Williams's deepest philosophical inquiry into the relationship between fiction and history. On one level, it presents historical narrative—a sequence of events and of facts that are little known to either scholars or the general public, but which can be verified. Incorporating documentary methods developed by previous writers like Dos Passos in his *U.S.A.* trilogy and Mailer in *The Naked and the Dead*, Williams incorporates into the novel speeches, government transcripts, diaries, letters, and fragments from histories as objective testimony as evidence to establish a verifiable chain of events. Yet in the very act of assembling this information and structuring it throughout the five major parts of the novel, Williams as a novelist involves himself in a second level of historiography. The novel itself is Williams's way of studying and interpreting these facts, in creating a fictional, highly critical narration that lends meaning to objective historic events.[10] The very act of fictive narration conveys the author's critique of history: Narrative fiction and narrative fact thus fuse, becoming mutually sustaining elements in the work. One lends credibility and a degree of objective consistency to events; the other postulates that in the novelistic re-creation of history, the most deeply hidden facts can be projected vividly and that—in terms of Williams's methods and the startling, somewhat ambiguous conclusion—anything is possible. In sum, the practice of historical fiction in *Captain Blackman* involves both corroborative chronicle and invention. Intent on presenting a vision of American history largely absent from both historical scholarship and fiction, Williams filters two hundred years of events through the mind of his hero who is once again "trapped by history" but who seeks a sort of dialectical release.

Whereas Conrad once observed that fiction is human history, Williams is more interested here in fiction as historical process. Historicity in the novel involves an effort on the author's art to explore the contemporary human condition through its relationship to the past. "The historical," wrote Hegel, "belongs to us only when we can see the present in general as a consequence of those events in the chain of which the characters or actions described constitute an essential link." We have seen this type of historical positivism at work in Williams's fiction from *Sissie* onward. For him there is a continuity to history: The present can be explained by the past and, in novels like *Sons of Darkness,*

Sons of Light and *Captain Blackman*, the present can also predict the future. Fiction transforms this dialectic, providing historical process with the reality of form that is needed to inscribe events with meaning. Fiction is the narrative vehicle through which history can be seen anew. Thus historical fiction becomes for Williams a mode of revelation, as well as a means of revenge—a way to salvage the past despite the best attempts of culture to destroy it or keep it hidden. Captain Blackman, as protagonist in the novel, embodies this hidden process. He is the historical and political consciousness in the novel, a figure who, finding himself "as in a dream" marching beside black revolutionary soldiers at the start of the book, is a historian with a prescribed educational mission. "You git in this dream with me and see what's really goin down," declares Blackman. "Dumb-ass niggers. Never learn nothin" (19). Blackman is Williams's persona. The novel itself is a bildungsroman, a necessary educational journey, because for Williams, failure to understand history is tantamount to cultural suicide.

Epic Fiction

In *Captain Blackman*, Williams presents history in epic proportions. In part, the novel is a modern *Iliad*, chronicling a nation's wars and telling of both base and heroic deeds. Blackman is the epic hero, a man who covers continents, fighting ironically for a nation that awards him only a captain's rank after two hundred symbolic years of combat. A primal figure, Blackman possesses almost immortal proportions. Always in the vanguard of the most nightmarish fighting in any war, he carries his unique identity to the extremes of human danger. At one stage, during World War I, he is even blown up, but experiences a miraculous resurrection. Receiving a direct bomb hit, Blackman sees his position reduced to a "gaping hole" with "only pieces of men left." His men work into the darkness, carrying away the shreds of bodies, until they come upon Blackman:

First they uncovered Blackman's head, sure it was all they'd find because of the angle at which it was stuck in the ground. But the neck came after then the shoulders, at still another angle, then the torso, arms intact, the pelvis and legs attached. He was alive and unmarked; the men who'd been on either side of him and in front and behind him had been blown to bits. (186)

Blackman transcends time, place, mortality. Even after the "concrete" Blackman of the Vietnam War period has been chewed apart—legs, testicles, trunk—by the AK-478s, he emerges, admittedly mutilated, from the sort of destruction that would have killed normal men.

To the extent that Blackman is a symbol both of the black man and the black soldier, and war is a paradigm of social and political conflict, we can understand the author's essential approach to his epic. Most revealing, in terms of Williams's conception of art and of history, *Captain Blackman* is an example of "epic fiction" in the Brechtian sense of the term. We are distanced from the protagonist by his larger-than-life proportions, but beyond this we are distanced from action by the very structuring of time. The novel's action, set simultaneously in the present and in the past, in the realm of conscious and unconscious time, is a primary distancing or "alienation" device that serves to destroy partially the fiction of illusion common to the realistic-naturalistic tradition. Stylistically, the work is exceedingly realistic in its depiction of men at war and of landscape in general. Moreover, Williams, like any serious novelist, wants us to enjoy the tale. Nevertheless, as with Brechtian theater, we never suspend disbelief, or permit ourselves to be swallowed by the illusion. We are constantly aware in *Captain Blackman* that the novel is an artifact— one where story is the essence of the work, but where intriguing aspects of the narrator's craft alert the audience to the lessons that must be drawn from the tale. As readers, we must contend intellectually with the historicity of the narrative and with Blackman as a historical type, as the consciousness of his race. Fully 90 percent of the novel is set in the past, a past that moves in a linear manner until it dovetails with the present. Thus the reading audience must be prevailed upon to treat action as material that is preeminently historical, and that—whether dramatized or melodramatized—offers historical truths.

The formal devices in *Captain Blackman* encourage readers to approach the novel as a historical document, a chronicling of events that must be scrutinized objectively. Action in each of the six major sections of the novel covers and re-creates blocks of American military history. Part 1 covers the Revolutionary War, the War of 1812, and the Civil War. Part 2 treats the Plains Wars and the Spanish-American War, ending with the Brownsville insurrection of August 3, 1906. Part 3 focuses on World War I, and Part 4, the shortest section in the novel, superlative in execution, invokes the Spanish Civil War. Part 5 concentrates on World War II, and Part 6 takes readers through the Korean War, the Vietnam War, and an imaginary future nuclear war during which covert black revolutionaries, sent by Blackman from the heart of Africa, triumph over the collective history of white, imperialistic militarism. Thus the structure is epic and historical, while the narrative, blending the factual and the fictive, offers episodic fables (Brecht used the German word *Fabel* to denote the didactic importance of the story line) on the meaning of American history. Throughout each major section, we perceive Blackman as a sort of embodied spirit or force incarnating history,[11] even as secondary characters, some of whom exist in actual present time, accompany him on his journey. Although we can make the plot seem probable by inferring that Blackman's subconsciousness, once activated, would deal with his waking preoccupations, the actual effect while reading the novel is not as much one of vicarious participation in the action, as it is an intellectual understanding of it.

Epic Technique

To objectify the historical dimension of the action, Williams uses a variety of distancing devices throughout the novel. Title pages for each of the six major parts contain prefatory material drawn from various primary historical sources. Focusing on the black American soldier and on the racial dilemma in the military that reflects the broader cultural malaise, these factual glosses help to establish the historicity of each part. For the title page of Part 1, Williams reproduces part of the 1832 testimony of John Chavis, one

of the many forgotten black American soldiers whom the
author resurrects in the course of the novel: "Tell them that
if I am Black I am free born American & a revolutionary
soldier & therefore ought not to be thrown intirely out of
the scale of notice" (11). Similarly, Part 4, the section of the
Spanish Civil War, contains on its title page a quote from
Arthur H. Landes on the Abraham Lincoln Brigade:

From the very beginning, the Abraham Lincoln Brigade was an integrated unit. The concepts of real freedom embodied in the
general antifascist philosophy of the men of the Lincoln Brigade
precluded any ideas of racial superiority, or minority discrimination. Such ideas were utterly alien to the men and represented, in
essence, the enemy they had come so far to fight. (191)

These title pages resemble the Brechtian theater devices of
signs, screens, and slides that preface scenes, alerting the audience to content and meaning, while simultaneously fram-
ing the fictional story with a primary distancing device.

Williams constantly disrupts the traditional fiction of illusion by varied alienation techniques. Italicized sections of
from one to five pages called Cadences appear throughout
Captain Blackman, serving as parables on the hidden
governments, composed of the military, economic, social,
and political elite who conspire to rule the world and subjugate various peoples and races. Like the chapter sketches
interspersed throughout Hemingway's *In Our Time*, these
vignettes magnify the meaning of their relevant sections.
Projecting policy makers in ludicrous but lethal postures, the
Cadences sections often fuse disparate tonalities, shading
toward the apocalyptic and the grotesque. In one Cadences
episode, placed within the World War II section, two scientists discuss the application of nuclear force in absurdist
tones: "This fission is a pain in the ass," declares one scientist. "Fusion, that's the answer, more power, less space.
Boom! Your hear me, Doctor, BA-roOM!" (241). In these
sections, Williams offers parables on both the evil and the
banality of a world as well as entire historical cycles governed by the basest human impulses.

Just as distortion and exaggeration control the form and
substance of the Cadences, "Drumtaps" sections offer mean-

ings for those who want to look at history microscopically in order to discover what dictates actual events. The Cadences are fiction rooted all too firmly and uncomfortably in historical fact and inferences; Drumtaps are the historical facts themselves—short primary documents alerting readers to the reality of events and corroborating the fictive narrative, especially for readers who do not understand the sinister overtones of our national heritage. Predominating in the Drumtaps are oral and written testimonies of men who have fought our nation's wars, from obscure soldiers to the famous and infamous. Occasionally, Williams juxtaposes two Drumtaps segments to offer historical problems that readers themselves must unravel. Here, for example, is a Drumtaps gloss on the role of the Rough Riders and their black counterparts, the Buffaloes, during the Spanish-American War:

Drumtaps

Negro soldiers were peculiarly dependent on their white officers . . . None of the white regulars or Rough Riders showed the slightest sign of weakening; but under the strain the colored infantrymen began to get a little uneasy and drift to the rear.

PRESIDENT THEODORE ROOSEVELT

If I am correctly informed as to the history of the Spanish-American War, it is reported that if it had not been for the gallant and courageous action of the Tenth Regiment of the Cavalry at the battle of San Juan we might not have the privilege of having in the White House that brave soldier and "square deal" and patriotic President of ours. As I understand, had it not been for the gallantry of the Tenth Regiment of Cavalry, a colored regiment, at that battle there might not have been a sufficient number of Rough Riders left to tell the tale.

SENATOR NATHAN B. SCOTT (131)

The Drumtaps demystify history. They serve both to objectify and corroborate the unpleasant presentation of military history that the author invokes so vividly in the narrative of Blackman's progress through the nation's wars.

Williams also reproduces fragments of primary source material in the main narrative as well as songs and popular lyrics. A piece of martial verse from the Revolutionary period captures the tenor of this material:

> The rebel clowns, ah what a sight
> Too awkward was their figure,
> 'Twas yonder stood a pious wight
> And here and there a nigger. (37)

Songs, poetry, black "toasts," and folk sayings rooted in oral tradition all serve to deepen cultural history and to reveal the contours of combat and the lessons learned from it. For the black soldier, participation in American wars placed him in a doubly alien environment: on the one hand, he had to fight his putative enemies, and on the other he had to survive in a world of intense racial hatred generated by his putative compatriots. The author incorporates every relevant device to orchestrate this point, to verify it, to force the reader to accept it. As such, he continues and amplifies the tradition of epic literature established by Brecht, who felt that unusual artistic devices were needed to convey the complexity of human and historical processes. Writing in 1931, Brecht had observed: "Today, when human character must be understood as the 'totality of all social conditions' the epic form is the only one that can comprehend all the processes, which could serve the drama as materials for a fully representative picture of the world." [12] In *Captain Blackman*, Williams fuses fact and fiction, using a variety of devices to achieve epic form. The novel does not approximate the socialist realism that Brecht aspired to in his work, but it does convey historical realism. Blackman's "cadences" and history's cadences are inseparable. Historical imperatives govern the real Blackman and the timeless Blackman, taking him ultimately, as Lawrence declared of the characters in *Moby Dick*, to the bottom of himself.

Blackman's Journey

Williams designs his protagonist's journey through history as an unsentimental education. Blackman is simultaneously participant, observer, commentator, and instructor during this odyssey. His quest is not so much for a romantic or spiritual artifact, for the Golden Fleece or the Holy Grail, as it is for the dialectic and the essential meaning of human experience through history. Blackman marches with history, from Lexington and Concord, to Valley Forge, to the battle of New Orleans, through the Civil War's racist horrors at Pillow and Pison Springs, through the New York Draft riots, the Brownsville Raid, the Houston riot, and beyond. At each stage of this pilgrimage, he is haunted by an omnipresent adversary, first appearing as a nameless aide to General Washington, and reminding Blackman

. . . of a serpent flowing back into itself as it is uncovered beneath a dead dog. The man's face seemed to float directly from his body, without a neck; this face, its eyes, locked with Blackman's and Blackman saw that it was whiter than any face he'd ever seen, and the eyes were space-blue, so that he felt as though he were looking into the center of nothingness. (40–41)

This officer named Whittman is actually "white-man": he is General Jackson, General Custer—all the imperial custodians of white supremacy in the nation's history.

Blackman knows the essence of these military men with their translucent blue eyes and flaxen hair. Of Custer, Williams writes: "The 10th [a black regiment] pinched the Indians against the Washita to await the arrival of Custer's forces which were to lead them to a reservation; instead the 7th slaughtered them, men, women and children" (108). The original Whittman is also the avatar of Major Whittman, the Vietnam contemporary of Blackman, the military incompetent with his "space-blue eyes" who nevertheless outranks his black counterpart and contrives to destroy him, as history has contrived to subjugate minorities in the American army. Blackman cannot shake Whittman's ominous presence. In Korea, Blackman physically beats his adversary, who cannot read a map properly, "clubbing him into the ground with his fists and loving it, but at times recoiling from the burning hatred in the blue eyes" (303). But like a serpent shedding its skin, Whittman uses the institutional forces available to him to survive and to remain in the army even as Blackman, after his recuperation, with the ceremonial bestowal of medals and higher rank, will be cashiered out at the age of forty.

American military history involves a continuing effort to exploit and then cashier out—either dead or alive—the black soldier. During the Revolutionary War, Blackman, already a leader of the motley band of largely unarmed blacks impressed to fight against the British, asks if freedom, twenty dollars, and a hundred acres of land await those who fight. The ambiguous but essentially negative answer is demonstrated by events and by the recorded racist observations of men like General Schuyler, one of the numerous actual figures whom Williams introduces. Similarly, blacks, Indians, and Creoles are conscripted to defend New Orleans against the British during the War of 1812. Griot, who travels with Blackman during actual and mythic time, knows the duplicity of the white officers demanding their allegiance: "It's down t de skinnin o de shrimp big man, an day gonna be askin us to fight; dey gonna say 'now lissen yall black fellers'—dey won't be callin us niggers t'morrow— 'dem Raidcoats is in de harbuh, dey is comin in here t take over Merica n youse black fellers is Mericans jes like de rest of us, so you got t he'p us fight.' Dey don said it befo n dey goan say it again, big Aper" (46). Conscripted to fight, the free blacks (but not the slaves) receive land for their services, but on February 18, 1820, in a document that Williams incorporates into the narrative, the Office of the Adjutant General declares: "No Negro or Mulatto will be received as a recruit of the Army" (57). From war to war and battlefield to battlefield, Williams carefully dramatizes and documents episodes that demystify much American military history, replacing the glory of warfare with a more somber confrontation with revealed fact. For Williams, and every serious novelist, historical fiction must reveal historical truth.

The essential historical truth in *Captain Blackman* involves a paradox that serves to define the author's political vision. Updating Aristotle's definition of politics, Williams demonstrates that men come into contact with each other, or form social institutions, because they need each other. Clearly, America's major wars could not have been fought tenaciously or successfully without black soldiers, the nearly two million individuals from the Revolutionary War to Vietnam, who suffered disproportionate casualties, including atrocities committed by white American troops and civilians. Yet the "good life" envisioned by Aristotle as the purpose of political groupings is a segregated notion, existing for the dominant race in America. The black soldier in American military history is a commodity. At the political level, he is both a problem and a pariah, excluded from the advantages enjoyed, as Williams declares through the dialogue of Andrew Jackson, under America's "mild and equitable government" (48).

Style

Critics and readers who think that Williams melodramatizes reality overlook the range of approaches the author develops to convey his thesis. Aside from the different rhythms of the Drumtaps and Cadences sections, Williams's style, his application of the syntactic possibilities of language, is broadly varied. At points, the style seems almost journalistic, as facts, filtered through the editorial mind of Captain Blackman, speak for themselves. Recording the Civil War atrocities at Fort Pillow, Williams writes: "General Nathan Bedford Forrest ordered the slaughter of three hundred black troops after they'd surrendered; they said the Mississippi, which flows fast and deep past Memphis, ran red with blood for two days, and that the black civilians fished out heads, arms, legs and torsos. . . ."(67). At other times, a hardboiled realism governs the author's presentation of battle sequences, as in this description of the deaths of two members of the Lincoln Brigade:

As though in slow motion, the two ran across the road, the signal flapping between them. Even as he was fixing his end in its final position, Pick clutched his stomach, then his chest and fell, the blue flashes winding steadily. Streisand dropped his end and ran to help him, but he too went down, and for a full five minutes, they were the targets of concentrated rifle and machine gun fire, the sounds of which seemed to have no relationship to the flashes. They were skinned by the bullets, flayed, disemboweled; almost no part of their bodies remained untouched; it was as though two huge piles of ground meat had been thrown down upon the road. (204–05)

Such description is not melodramatic, for it does not sentimentalize death; instead, the very duration of the enemy firing conveys a moral judgment against those who reduce humanity to mounds of flesh.

Where Williams actually does employ melodrama is in highly stylized scenes that unfold like a ballet, pitting the white world against the black at the level of symbol and myth. Two episodes illuminate this style. The first is in chapter 6, where Blackman rapes a southern white woman, already kept by a Union officer, before the gagged and bound white man. Here, Williams plays with white and black psychosexual myths (a motif that would dominate his next novel, *Mothersill and the Foxes*), fashioning them to fit Blackman's desire for revenge. The scene is not melodrama in the traditional sense; although the action is exaggerated almost to the point of the ludicrous, it is not sentimentalized, for meaning enhances melodramatic method. As a second example, Williams in chapter 20 melodramatizes history itself by creating the Tombolo incident, where 200 black soldiers and their Italian women desert the army during World War II, making a last stand in the swamps, where all are ultimately liquidated. Blackman is witness to this hidden dimension of history, one that has never been substantiated as fact, but which emerged as rumor and inference during the author's research for the novel. In the sequence of events centering on Tombolo, Williams melodramatizes action to underscore a central thesis in the book—that the American military establishment's methods of liquidation historically have been embraced by black American soldiers themselves. Functional or organic melodrama, rather than the conventional variety largely devoid of meaning, is simply one of many devices Williams develops.

Probably the most troublesome stylistic and structural aspect of *Captain Blackman* is the conclusion. Williams creates a futuristic vision of an American nuclear military establishment, presided over by the ubiquitous General Whittman, that has been infiltrated by light-skinned blacks who have incapacitated the entire system. Blackman, from a clandestine base in the heart of Africa, has masterminded the downfall of the white race, Soviet and American alike. Here the writing moves much closer to the fantastic or the grotesque than other scenes in the novel, requiring yet another adjustment in terms of readers' perceptions of tonality. Basically, they must avoid the temptation to treat the conclusion as an actual grotesque vision of the future, rather than the last of Blackman's reveries. Read carefully, the novel indicates that Blackman is still sleeping, with "the most incredible smile on his face" (332) as his hideous vision of the future unfolds. Blackman moves out of the weighted past into a vision of the future as a sort of historical vindication.

Williams spent a great deal of time on the conclusion, revising it at the request of the Doubleday editors. "When I turned in *Captain Blackman*, what are now the final two chapters were one long chapter. Some people at Doubleday felt that the material was too powerful to be in one chapter. My first response to separating them was, no. I liked it the way it was. Then I looked at it again. If I set it apart, the conclusion would be even more powerful. So I agreed."[13] The novel ends on a powerfully distorted note. Williams's vision of an involuted world turned upside down in terms of racial power is the final distancing technique that he employs to induce readers to examine carefully the terrifying patterns of history. He intimates that a bizarre and lethal future awaits nations and races that perpetuate forms of racial oppression and exploitation. The history of Western civilization seems to take a familiar route toward conquest of all Third World people. Yet Williams implies ironically that our last destination might turn out to be in a strange land governed by historical reversals. All the world indeed could be sad and dreary, but this time for the white race.

Chapter Seven

Affirmations: *Mothersill and the Foxes* and *The Junior Bachelor Society*

John Williams arrived at artistic maturity when, in the novels of his second phase, he made political and historical realities the center of his fiction. Yet the main characters in his next two novels after *Captain Blackman* are not determined by the overbearingly political nature of existence; basically, they seek nonpolitical or apolitical vantage points in their efforts to operate successfully in the world. Abandoning political reality as the shaping spirit of his fiction, in *Mothersill and the Foxes* (1975) and *The Junior Bachelor Society* (1976) Williams creates a new artistic sensibility, working to define fresh qualities in the American character. For him, this sensibility involves the search for personal affirmations. His characters now seek private rather than political or collective peace. They prefer simple versions of social commitment and respond increasingly to gentler, even pastoral, rhythms in the American landscape.

With the composition of Williams's seventh novel, *Mothersill and the Foxes*, the author apparently had reached an impasse in the development of his craft. Beginning as raucous parody of black sexuality, *Mothersill and the Foxes* shifts to a disparate series of narrative forms and points of view; it ends ultimately as a pastoral fairy tale with its hero, a wounded but repaired Fisher King, at peace with the fertility of the natural world. What we witness in this novel is an author contending with a potentially important theme, finding significant surface motifs and resonances in it, but failing

116

ultimately in the attempt to create a satisfactory vehicle for the content. In terms of Williams's artistic development, the seriocomic approach to the problems of the protagonist, Odell Mothersill, is a necessary preparation—something perhaps that the author had to get out of his system—for the more challenging and successful affirmations awaiting characters in future novels. Williams operates unevenly in new fictive territory in *Mothersill and the Foxes*. Nevertheless, we can see in this novel a preparation for the return to an austere, carefully crafted realism at the heart of his eighth novel, *The Junior Bachelor Society*.

The Myth of Black Sexuality

Mothersill and the Foxes is an ironically inverted presentation of the myths of black sexuality. Odell Mothersill is that peculiar variety of American innocent, thoroughly experienced in sexual lore, who wants to offer women his essential goodness, but who fails and consequently remains, in his forties, uncertain of his masculinity. Odell's sexual odyssey began when he was seduced by his babysitter at the age of nine, from which point his experiences served to define the contours of his adolescence and his adult life. He pursues and is pursued by "foxes." He is the hunter and the hunted, seeking fulfillment through sex. Endowed with remarkable phallic strength, Mothersill is the prototypical cocksman, "a small god" as he is described during his pubescent affair with the babysitter, who tries to offer "pure benevolence" to all his partners.[1] As a social worker and later as a Peace Corps administrator, he merges vocation and avocation, dispensing with his sexual largesse in city and suburb, at home and abroad, over a period of time spanning the Depression and the late 1960s.

Odell Mothersill is well-educated, urbane, professional. He is a man with a social conscience. He is warm and humane but ultimately narcissistic, unable to transcend egotism. Through his own perverse assertions of will, he is guilty of a series of failures with women that hound him into his early forties. For Mothersill's ego is his penis. This sexual pride shatters the lives of women who come into contact with him, turning them toward insanity, suicide, lesbianism, and

other radical alternatives or self-destructive acts. Toward the
end of the novel, Mothersill's sexual excesses catch up with
and overwhelm him; on the verge of unwittingly marrying
his own daughter, a hip young activist of the 1960s, he is
wounded with bullets fired by the mother, one of his many
former lovers. Thus purged, Mothersill can prepare himself
for marriage to a new woman, fatherhood, and life in a rural
retreat.

This brief overview indicates the thematic continuity
governing the novel's development. While Mothersill's exploits and dilemmas move the action forward, however, the
novel is not altogether successful. Parts of it are daring, filled
with superb stylistic and structural improvisations. The first
of the six major parts contains some of Williams's finest
writing; in it he offers a series of juxtaposed bizarre scenes, a
fictive gambit best adjusted to short fiction that is always difficult to sustain. *Mothersill and the Foxes* is thereafter only
intermittently a grotesque novel. Whereas the quality of
Mothersill's world in the first section is established by the
author's inquiring intelligence and ability to create absurdist
fiction, succeeding sections—measured against the first—
lose their comic zest, and much of Williams's insight into
human sexuality dissipates in generalization, contrivance,
and melodrama. One senses an artist trying to maintain intense imaginative involvement with his subject, gradually
losing interest, and then moving in a mechanical, somewhat
contrived way toward an optimistic conclusion. As such, the
affirmative vision at the end of the novel loses a degree of
validity.

What we do have is the remarkable first section, a panorama of sexuality throughout the novel, and—perhaps of
equal significance—a perceptible conflict within Williams as
an imaginative artist attempting to break away from the
political themes of his second phase. He experiments here
with fictional modes close to those employed by such contemporaries as Roth, Pynchon, and Ellison, yet retreats finally
(as an important motif in the novel indicates) to realism. As
such, *Mothersill and the Foxes* is a transitional novel in
which Williams experiments with absurdist fiction and with
the possibility of creating a black Portnoy before returning
to more traditional modes.

The absurd or grotesque tone arising from the vagaries of
sexual behavior in the contemporary world appears at the
outset of the novel as Mothersill, in a keen state of sexual anticipation, escorts a barmaid named Shirley, possessor of
"the biggest tits in the world" (13), to his Greenwich Village
apartment. Soon they are naked on the living room rug. The
television flickers aimlessly. Mothersill is ready for sex but at
that very moment Shirley's favorite program, "Cheyenne,"
is announced. As Mothersill, cast immediately as a mock
hero, quickly loses his sexual ardour, Shirley proceeds to
couple vicariously with her favorite media he-man:

"Kick his ass, Cheyenne! Whump! Aw, do it, Cheyenne!" She
paused between exclamations to smile at Mothersill. He, however,
was willing his limp penis to rise, but the flesh was weak, mor-
tified, and unable to sustain the imagery. Finally it sulked between
his thighs as if seeking a hiding place. (18)

Shirley is television's bride, and Mothersill's impotence
becomes the ironic emblem of the scorned human lover.
Sated by television, Shirley nevertheless is willing now to accommodate Mothersill, but he is unable to meet any
feminine challenge to his wilted manhood. The two trade insults, doing the dozens. Shirley then walks out, leaving
Mothersill with the first in a series of debilitating defeats.

Williams moves from keen parody of sexuality at the start
of the novel to equally comic renditions of Mothersill's affairs with the babysitter and with his sister as an adolescent;
after-hours intercourse with a co-worker named Annabelle;
autoerotic boyhood practices in the attic; sex among the
proper members of his boyhood community in Cleveland;
sex with a welfare client; sex at a voyeuristic orgy involving
two of Annabelle's roommates. In all these episodes,
Williams's satiric-parodic method shifts skillfully through
various ranges of the grotesque; episodes are ludicrous but
they are also potentially alienating and ultimately horrifying.

Williams stresses the duality of the comic and the serious
throughout Part 1. Mothersill's antics in attempting to serve
all women has a serious correspondence in his efforts to ease
the suffering of the world's body as symbolized in its
children. Possessing an apprehension of the ideal—even

ideal love—he is forced to contend instead with insinuated signs of abandonment, betrayal, isolation, violence, and perversion—human passions and characteristics lurking beneath the comic surface of the narrative. This duality in the very fabric of life turns Mothersill into an individual with an eye for the grotesque. For instance, as a twenty-five-year-old social worker in 1950, he sees the faces of his caseload in stark, heightened outlines: "They clawed at him without so much as raising their voices or lifting their eyes. He saw in their stunted black, brown and white bodies even in his sleep, scribblings by Daumier" (30).

Allusions to art, television, photography, and other media constitute a significant motif in *Mothersill and the Foxes*. Here and in the pages immediately following are lurid and bizarre scenes—of children eaten alive by rats, or of one where a "mother and a lover, drunkenly fornicating on a floor, kept vigil over a baby on the couch three days dead" (31). Images of grotesque humanity reveal a thematic center of reduced, almost demonic existence in the modern world. When Annabelle's roommates, Marilyn and Marge, offer themselves as edibles during the orgy toward the end of the first section, we see them as disembodied and dehumanized souls, grotesquely frozen caricatures in a mixed media spectacle: "He saw five figures, whose whiteness was heightened by the blue glare of the lamp. None were facing him; they were a freize brought to life, complete with small sounds, of sudden sibilant utterances, *Greeks and Romans Busy at Orgy*; they moved slowly upon the entablature of bedroom floor prolonging their pleasures" (60). By this time, Williams's satire on collective sex as self-consuming ritual has become ominous and eerie. In the last scene of Part 1, Marilyn and Marge are found hacked to pieces, split open like beef from neck to vagina. A policeman's comment while viewing this grisly scene—"'Everything but toast and hamburger buns'" (64)—suggests the "grotesque in horror" absolutely alien from humanity that Poe himself defined as the essence of his art. Williams's own mockery is terrible: sex is no longer simply a joke to be laughed at easily. With savage irony, he leaves Mothersill at the end of this section as impotent as he was at the beginning. In this last sinister scene, the terrors of our most demonic selves have throttled the hero's lofty sexual flights.

Whereas Part 1 of *Mothersill and the Foxes* encapsulates Williams's craftsmanship in handling complex narrative perspectives and tones, the subsequent sections reject this complexity for more standard fictional approaches. There is still a comic element, but Williams tends to engage more in self-conscious reflections on the failure of human sexuality in the modern world. He rejects the contemporary assumption that sex is salvation. In Part 2, for example, which is largely devoid of humor, Mothersill's serious affair with Eunice Potts founders on her perforated hymen and her mental breakdown. Part 3, set in the Caribbean, involves Mothersill in a series of contrived episodes centering on a native nymphomaniac, a kinky millionaire couple, and an old girlfriend who has graduated from heterosexuality to lesbianism; here the annihilation of all human values because of sexuality is a somber theme that dampens any potentially ludicrous overtones. Parts 4 and 5, which have as their thematic focus the civil rights movement of the late 1960s, contain a fundamental sense of social and sexual exhaustion. The episodic sixth section, entitled "Chapter One," treats Mothersill's surprising regeneration after he is shot. A new woman, Marie, walks into his life and they retreat to the country. Mothersill, a father-to-be, suddenly is a rural pied piper, waiting for two boys and two girls that they have adopted from foster homes. Thus from the critique of the ill-formed world in the first section of the novel, Williams seems to set progressively smaller fictive goals for himself and to stick to artificial surfaces rather than the deep seriocomic structure with which he began.

Nevertheless, Williams did conceive *Mothersill and the Foxes* in large and significantly structured terms, and there are themes in the novel that confirm such intentions. One key element in the interior design is the imagery related to art, notably the allusions to Millet's familiar painting *The Sower*. Williams was prepared at the outset to grapple with serious social, psychological, and esthetic problems through this art motif. Mothersill is an ironically inverted sower, his life transformed into intense philosophical and artistic drama. Early in the novel, Williams writes:

When he slept at night he dreamed he was Millet's *The Sower* striding across a brown, plowed field, his hat pulled down on his head, his right hand clutching the seed in his bag, about to spray it forward fall into the furrows. His grain sack, like the sower's, dangled from his left shoulder and his thick right leg, planted firmly on the softened ground, pushed ahead of his left, already raising behind him . . . .There was nothing in the sower's manner to indicate that he would not be able to bring forth new life from the earth over whose bosom and bottom he strode. Nothing. (32)

"Nothing" is the emblem of Mothersill's world. Williams's frequent allusions to grotesque art especially capture the reduction, distortion, and emptiness in Mothersill's life. For instance, Mothersill dreams after his Caribbean adventure with Margo Purchase, the lesbian, that he is a sower "in pure Corot lines, a face starkly drawn, heavily lashed and rouged" (164). At best, as in Williams's handling of the Millet motif, we sense a writer attempting to both create new vehicles to explain the enigmatic features of human sexuality and to provide a full formulation of the methods of making fiction.

Mothersill embodies a new consciousness in Williams's work. He is the hero who rejects the larger social and political problems of the times and seeks more promising alternatives. He reduces existence to a rural idyll in which he can adopt children, enjoy love, sex, and procreation, and luxuriate in the wealth of nature—the "sounds of summer—the screaming jays, the pigeons in the old barn, the peeps of the hawks, the distant barks of dogs, the hiss of young wind through the trees" (239). Williams in *Mothersill and the Foxes* withholds the hecatomb that marks his previous fiction. He provides absolution instead of apocalypse, even as Mothersill is made to suffer. After paying for his indiscriminate sowing, Mothersill merges with the most timeless of myths, oneness with uncorrupted nature. At the end of the novel, he does become the fruitful sower, and his newfound procreative inclinations enable him for the first time in his life to minister to the orphans of the world.

This Sporting Life

While *Mothersill and the Foxes* was for Williams a unique but only partially successful experiment, the author's strengths in conceiving and executing significant novelistic structures crystallize perfectly in *The Junior Bachelor Society* (1976). In his eighth novel, a group of men are approaching the age of fifty—Ralph, Bubbles, Dart, Chops, Shurley, Clarie, Snake, Cudjo, and Moon. They attend a reunion in their hometown honoring the seventieth birthday of their high school coach, Charles "Chappie" Davis. Some, like Bubbles Wiggins, who works (as Williams once did) in a foundry, and Kenneth "Snake" Dumpson, a housing commissioner, still live in Central City, the author's fictional embodiment of Syracuse. Others have crossed the continent and the globe, assuming professional lives as academics, playwrights, journalists, or concert singers. All in this beautifully orchestrated novel are middle-class representatives—from the solid blue-collar worker to the entrenched mildly activist college English professor. No one, however, has enjoyed unadulterated success. In fact, only one, Walter "Moon" Porter, a Los Angeles pimp, seems capable of handling the world on its own terms, of manipulating crises and forging a new life and a new identity for himself. Moon, the most unusual and thoroughly accomplished individual in Williams's long repertoire of professionals, knows how to control America's penchant for violence. Moon arrives uninvited for the reunion. He is Chance or Necessity, offering his former childhood friends what is tantamount to a middle-aged epiphany.

Again the political urgency that motivated Williams's best fiction in the 1960s and early 1970s is not apparent in *The Junior Bachelor Society*. The author, refining his treatment of middle-class life, presents instead the social concerns and patterns emerging from key relationships among the Bachelors, their wives, and the outside world. The novel thus represents a quick departure also from the extreme and somewhat trendy universe of *Mothersill and the Foxes* and a return to the vivid social textures of *Sissie*. The Bachelors and their wives, converging on Central City for the three-day reunion after having been separated for more than thirty years, are survivors, and Williams takes considerable care to create them in finely crafted, exquisitely varied profiles.

There is a certain degree of melodramatic violence, for which Williams has always had a penchant, in the odyssey of Moon, who must kill a crooked policeman early in the novel and then eliminate another to save the Junior Bachelor Society. But these carefully controlled tableaus are used as frame devices to enable Williams to state his theme about the need to transcend, often through rebellious action, the social institutions that tend to exploit people. Central to his task is the portrayal of the psychological identities and social roles of a group of people, united in remembrance but discrete entities nevertheless, who come to middle age in America, changing even as the nation changes, but affected by the same latent social tensions that they have contended with all their lives. Written when Williams himself was nearing fifty, this is a recapitulation, deeply personal, of the passages in people's lives, and of forces that inevitably define their ability to love, hate, struggle and survive, and make sense of their lives.

Perhaps because *The Junior Bachelor Society* is one of the most intensely personal statements by the author (he actually seems to be a composite of several characters in the novel), the way Williams depicts character has special richness to it. As in no earlier novel, he sees his characters from within, especially in the first half of the book. Thus their personalities achieve a luminosity, precision, and energy that offers us access to the entire range of their behavior. Williams presents his characters with warmth and delicacy, brilliantly structuring the novel around shifting centers of consciousness. Starting with Bubbles, he introduces the Bachelors sequentially—singly, in pairs, in clusters. The novel builds by accretion, character upon character, individual life superimposed upon other lives, until everyone, as in the vast social tapestries of nineteenth-century fiction, is wed in a communal dilemma: what to do about Moon. For Moon is the cataclysmic presence hovering over their celebration. The Bachelors, paying homage to Chappie and through him to their own lives, must deal also with the blunter realities of existence, notably the fact that they are growing old.

Aging, memory, inheritance, that complex of features and values that people carry with them throughout time, contribute to the wistful, introspective quality of the prose. All the characters mix present and past, trying to recapture the communal spirit of their childhood through the ritual of the reunion. They know the penalties that time exacts, but all make exertions against time and aging, not without compromise, but perhaps with the intention of retaining their resilience and their hold on the patterns of their lives. In the first chapter, for example, Bubbles Wiggins (who shares with Moon a focal point in the novel) recalls the years, the seasons, the love and work of his life. This is one of the finest evocations of character and place in the entire body of Williams's fiction. It is autumn, and the strictly regulated span of action is predicated on this lingering time of year. Looking out the window of his house in a stolidly professional middle-class neighborhood, Bubbles takes pride in his status, sensing preconsciously the interpenetration of present and past, the living and the moribund: "Maples—soft, hard, royal, and Japanese—flared yellow and red against the clear sky; poplars, golden now, angled like spearheads, stood unbending and slender in contrast to the great twisting oaks. He missed the chestnut trees, their acrid smell and broad-veined leaves. Blight, they said, had killed them all." [2] Even as Bubbles muses about missed opportunities, he is essentially a celebrant of life, a man who feels good about himself, his family, his friends, his surroundings. In fact, the rhythms in this first chapter, notably contained in the superbly crafted depiction of Bubbles as he goes through the process of core-making at the foundry, are those of contemporary pastoral. Bubbles, as the center of the world depicted in the novel, indeed the person in charge of arranging the reunion for Coach Davis, is the man in motion: "He made a life, pounded it out of this sand and steel" (7). His greatest joy, however, is football, and he thinks of life as a game, made of rules that cannot be transgressed and that provide clear boundaries for success or failure. In the novel, sport activities are the metaphors of existence itself, rituals that serve as thematic and structural properties within the plot.

At least three of the Bachelors—Bubbles, Shurley, and Cudjo—still play Saturday football together, testing time and their corporeal beings, still delighting in their moves and cuts, the well-thrown pass, the straining toward the goal

line. The Jefferson Park area where they play, described in
the second chapter, is now a totally black neighborhood; it
has changed from the days when blacks, Jews, and Italians
(the identical mix of Williams's own Fifteenth Ward in
Syracuse) ringed it. The teenagers who now watch the aging
Bachelors, wondering what the old jocks are up to, do not
sense the need to sustain the communal bond. Intertwined
with the sense of community is the personal joy that sports
continue to bring to the Bachelors' lives. Williams filters this
joy through Bubbles, drinking his beer at Cudjo's bar after
the game, savoring his three touchdowns: "Once again he
watched himself driving over the field for each of those
touchdowns, saw each of his moves as clearly as if they'd
been filmed and halted frame after frame. He'd beat time out
on that field, whipped his ass good" (15). The game actually
involves multiple contests, all rooted in a deceptive ecstasy,
in the imagined ability to transcend time or to turn it back to
the vitality of youth.

In their youth, the Bachelors had used sports as deliver-
ance from the ghetto. Sports was their gimmick, their ticket
out of a constricted social world. James Baldwin, in *The Fire
Next Time*, observed that every black child "realizes, at
once, profoundly, because he wants to live, that he stands in
great peril and must find, with speed, a 'thing,' a gimmick, to
lift him out, to start him on his way." Many of the Bachelors
were started on their way by sports and by the careful super-
vision of Chappie Davis. They are part of a larger sports
mystique extending from every child who ever played ball to
those who became legendary professionals. Williams persistently equates strength and resilience of character with the
great black athletes of an earlier generation. Disciplined by
sport, these professionals used their physical abilities to
assault a system of segregation and separation that once embraced virtually all institutions including athletics. As
Clarence Henderson, once a black All American at Morris
Brown and now a college teacher, tells Moon during their
flight from California to the reunion, sports was a means of
mobility, "a way up and maybe a way out" (87). Survival
and success through sports, however, is not so compellingly
simple. Everything is won at cost, and historically the great

black athletes profitted the least from their abilities. Ironically, the best athlete among the Bachelors was Moon, who never went to college, and whose success story is based not so much on honoring the rules of the game as on manipulation of the rules of an exploitative culture in an effort to take advantage of society's own shortcomings. Moon, like all the Bachelors, is a product of the Depression, and he understands better than anyone in the novel that sport is the primal game: America itself is a contest, a war between the haves and have nots. A figure of power and authority, Moon is a person who understands that the sporting life is endemic in American culture, and that the strongest and the most willful and cunning are the ones who win the game.

Consequently, the joy of sports is tempered by certain ethical imperatives, including the recognition that athletic confrontations throwing black and white players together heighten racial struggles to almost epic proportions. Sport is national epic precisely because it is a concentrated representation of American life, containing the same tensions within its play structure as those existing in the outer world. Chappie Davis, waiting for Sundays, anticipating the cozy warmth of televised football, is both the reflector and moral arbiter of this shifting world of game and reality. A veteran of both the urban world and the sports universe, Chappie at seventy is a man for whom life, reduced to a simple set of outings and joyful anticipations, is like the patterns of a game. Viewing an offensive series by the Miami Dolphins, he reflects: "*See that*? It's the same way those cracker schools play ball, now they got some black players on their squads. Ole Morris ran that ball all the way down to the five and they send for Kiick to take it in. Peckerwoods!'" (42). To win, Chappie knows, one must defeat more than another team, for multiple conflicts are involved in winning or losing the game. In fact, the perimeters of sport reflect the boundaries in culture itself.

Conflict in sports, as in life, is a struggle for supremacy, an attempt to subdue an opposing force, to intimidate and defeat an antagonist. At a symbolic level, it involves matters of life and death. Even within a team, conflict permeates the lives of the players. Moon was the master of conflict as a young

player for the Junior Bachelor Society not only because he
was the best among them, but because he had a talent for
detecting and exploiting weaknesses in his friends, notably
the fear in Snake Dumpson. Sports thus test the human spirit,
pitting the contestants against each other and often against
the strengths and limitations of the self. The metaphorical
power deriving from sports is based on this idea that play
mirrors life as a fundamental conflict.

The Bachelors are not strangers to conflict in their adult
lives, or to private and public defeat. The lessons taught
them by Coach Davis, however, lessons rooted in the sports
philosophy of courage, stoicism, balance of mind and body,
and grace under pressure, provide a continuous sustaining
thread in their lives. In fact, the theme of continuity, of a
tradition of strength in conflict that is fostered by virtue and
brotherhood, is built into *The Junior Bachelor Society*. The
past informs the present in a special, poignantly human way
in this novel precisely because past acts are humanizing and
ritualistic, civilizing agents born out of human struggle.
Clarence Henderson, for example, likes to recall and recount
to his students the days of struggle for young black artists,
and how older artists like Langston Hughes would advise
them "that there would be rough water ahead, white water.
Clarence liked to relate these incidents to his students, for
they indicated a continuity they did not believe the black artist had" (50–51). Even as the lives of the Bachelors are arenas
of conflict, Chappie provides the thread of continuity; he is
the surrogate father and the protector, the one who in-
culcates the struggle to survive and the will to succeed.
Basically, then, the Bachelors are returning to Chappie in
order to seek reaffirmation of their lives and new inspira-
tion. Most are beset by difficulties, either in their professional lives, their marriages and relationships, or both.
Clarence Henderson, comfortably tenured at a California
university, has known guilt, frustration, and a sense of self-
betrayal in his marriage and professional life. Like the other
Bachelors, he embarks on a quest back to the source, seeking
in the reunion a return to a sacred circle in time, a new con-
secration of his spirit so that the present moment will once
again seem worthwhile.

Informed by the metaphors and symbolism of sport, *The Junior Bachelor Society* portrays these nine aging men as existential players who are not performing at their optimal levels. Most of them no longer can experience the brotherhood of a team; most find themselves in potentially alien fields of play. Even at the physical level, there are threatening agents: Cudjo Evers, working in the foundry with Bubbles, exists on Seconal, contending with a herniated disc that is hastening the end of his working days. Kenneth Dumpson, the housing commissioner with his white chauffeur and white wife, has tried to break the pattern, so that he has little left in common with the old neighborhood except a lingering rapport with Bubbles, his main man, the moral center of the Bachelors' fractured universe. Ezzard "Chops" Jackson, torn continually "between weariness and fury," is stuck as an executive at a black publications company, yoked to an unfaithful wife, a cuckolded overseer on the plantation. D'Artagnon Foxx, now an expatriate concert singer moving in a confused bisexual world, wanders between shifting realms of sexuality and culture, sliding down toward the end of his career. Ralph Joplin, Jr., resurrected from *Sissie* (along with Big Ralph and Iris) is a successful playwright, but he still does not have the stature that would enable him to prevent directors, producers, and theater owners from tampering with his plays. Atomized, held together by memories and occasional news about each other, the Bachelors have reached a point in midlife passage where they must take stock of themselves to retrieve their roots and their communal bond. Ralph thinks: "Could you transcend a quarter of a century, relate to the Depression, welfare, jockstraps, touchdowns, home runs, and baskets? Still there was cement to it all. Chappie. And quite probably more: the shared experience. They had all survived this city, to them the nation, the world, the universe" (93–94). All these men seem to apprehend that they are seeking in the reunion an affirmation transcending the limitations of their single selves and their present lives.

The Bachelors, bulwarks of Chappie's 1940–1943 Overlook High teams that won citywide championships in football, basketball, and track, functioned as a cohesive, organic team. As a special group, they seemed to live on a higher plane of existence, participating in "the shared experience," in the communality that developed through the obliteration of the individual identity into a magical unity of souls. While they have memories of this transcendental experience to sustain them, there are others excluded from this magical universe who developed little sense of team spirit or of community. These are the people whom Williams assails as the assassins of the human estate. Swoop Ferguson, a local cop who was never part of the Bachelors, is one. He is an isolate, a morally incapacitated individual. He is the counterpart of the crooked detective in Los Angeles whom Moon inadvertantly kills. Swoop is also shaking down his local constituency, including Shurley Walker, the secret owner of a restaurant and lounge. Moreover, it is Swoop who discovers the bulletin alerting police to arrest Moon and who pockets it, intending to exploit the knowledge by capturing Moon if he arrives for the reunion. Alienated from the Bachelors and from the older black generation typified by Chappie, indeed from society itself, Swoop is the psychotic mentality cut off from community and all higher forms of consciousness; he is a dangerous, potentially violent annihilator of values who must be killed by Moon at the end of the novel.

Violence and aggression are either latent or manifest components in human behavior, and also in most organized sports; and football is the paradigmatic sports activity that celebrates and ritualizes violence, even as it attempts to limit and define violence if only by the rules of the game. Thus it is appropriate that Williams elevates football in the novel as the key emblem of human behavior. Indeed, he sets the action in the football season, permitting the sport to serve as the best measure of conflict and brotherhood. Whereas physical violence is limited, almost exorcised in the celebratory Saturday football skirmishes participated in by three of the Bachelors, all the members retain uneasy memories of the power they once had to engineer destruction on and off the playing field. As adults, only Moon, the primal destroyer, has retained the destructive skills and abilities that had made him such a dominant force in football during his youth. When Henderson accidentally encounters Moon aboard a jet bound for New York, he immediately connects Moon with acts of violence:

That face, the calculating smile upon it, and Henderson recalling a Saturday afternoon when he had intercepted, cut for the sidelines, the high school crowd on its feet, and the October sun gleaming on Moon's helmet (no face guards then); the safety man angling over to pick them up, and Moon, the sun burnishing his helmet to gold, seeming to gather up, draw all his moving parts together, delivered himself like a shot from a sling, low, perfectly low—not a running block, but a killing block—knee-high, and took out the safety with a sound heard all over the field, a sound accompanied by the dull crack heard only by the three of them. A shattered fibula, the safety sprawling with a scream, he and Moon trucking over the goal line. (84)

With his helmet set ablaze by the sun, Moon is recalled as a mythic force. Indeed, the Bachelors, having heard about his profession, have not tried hard to locate him for the reunion; nevertheless they remember Moon as a special presence in their lives. Moon was a man-child who could use his mind and body in perfect harmony to vanquish opponents, whether on the playing fields or in the equally ritualistic seduction of girls for whom the Bachelors were contending.

Moon—this powerful, devastating figure who could have been a greater "success" than all the other Bachelors, but who through quirks and accidents is a success only in the shadowy world of American criminal culture—exists in a realm penetrated continually by violence. Even as he dislikes violence, in fact is tired of his profession as a pimp and wants to get out, he uses violence to kill. As the noted social critic and theologian Jacques Ellul, has explained, "The first law of violence is continuity. Once you start using violence, you cannot get away from it. Violence expresses the habit of simplification of situations, political, social, or human. And a habit cannot quietly be broken."[3] Moon is a man of violent habits, but he is also a man seeking release from violence. Thus Williams has somewhat ambivalent feelings about him. He does not want to condone violence or accept it as something inevitable and unavoidable in the conditioning process, but he does want to distinguish between the unjustified

violence of the corrupt Los Angeles detective or the institutionalized violence employed by Swoop, and the justifiable
violence of Moon. In this connection, the metaphor of sport
once again is relevant. Within the contours of sports activity,
the legitimizing of violence can occur. Thus the confrontation between Detective Collins and Moon at the start of the
novel is like a gladitorial contest, a physical combat won by
Moon, who clubs his rival into unconsciousness and in-
advertently, death. Similarly, there is a contest at the end of
the novel between the Bachelors, who want to protect
Moon, and Swoop, who intrudes into their party at Bubbles's
house to arrest Moon. The Bachelors at fifty are not cham-
pions of violence, but they do pull together to try to achieve
one last victory. They think mistakenly that Swoop can be
neutralized by incriminating tapes that Shurley has kept of
the periodic payoffs to Swoop and by cash that Moon offers
him as a stalling tactic. Moon, however, knows the laws and
the game of violence much better than the other Bachelors,
and he liberates both himself and the Bachelors by killing
Swoop before escaping to Canada and ostensibly a new life.

Moon is a figure capable of altering the rules of the game.
He is a person who rekindles temporarily the love and
solidarity once sensed by the Bachelors. He is one of the
most vivid and intriguing figures in Williams's fiction.
Drawn in the rich, somewhat flamboyant lines of characters
in the fiction of Chester Himes, he is a new figure—the
supreme player—in the body of Williams's work. Moon is
the criminal as good man, the figure who inverts unethical
structures in order to make them moral. Life is a contest for
Moon, and thus it requires, as in sport, certain strategies for
victory. Very much in the contemporary tradition of the
criminal as folk hero, Moon is astonished by the naive attempts of the Bachelors to save him, for he knows more
about coercion and about how to play out his hand than they
do. Moon becomes the rebel who legitimizes violence and
who tries to equalize the distance between the powerful and
the powerless. His choices, his strategies for playing the
game, do not involve painful moral choices. He does not
merely remain passive in the face of evil. Instead, he
legislates within the arena of his own activity against ex-
cessive violations of the rules of the game.

Moon's violent acts, coming as they do at the start and end of the novel, frame his more passionate desire to enjoy the fruits of success and to gain a new, simplified life. Moon wants to practice his own brand of virtue; he wants to settle down with his main woman in Canada and perhaps run a hunting lodge in the country. He is, in essence, another Mothersill, seeking rural peace. Williams interjects the pastoral motif into the novel when describing Moon's trip by car from New York City to the reunion upstate. It is one of the finest, most deftly resonant episodes in the novel. Stopping at a lodge in the mountains, he encounters Heflin, the black owner and proprietor who is a double of himself. Heflin has made the successful break, seeking final triumph and redemption in the natural world. In the end, Moon is also capable, because of his romanticized and mythic nature, to escape the lethal games of the world and to achieve pastoral transformation.

For the Bachelors as a group, they have experienced the flash of community and brotherhood, perhaps for the last time. They have acted with a single will, drawn painfully back into the team matrix, united in opposition to Swoop. They enjoy the very real achievement of strength through fellowship. But this last game is an exhausting contest, and the ritual of the weekend reunion has illuminated fears, weaknesses, and deficiencies in most of the Bachelors and their wives. Significantly, the last paragraph in the novel moves from Moon's liquidation of Swoop and his escape back to the Bachelors back to Bubbles, who returns us to the social and moral center of Williams's middle-class universe:

Bubbles, sitting at the head of the table, thought he heard a car backfiring way off in the distance; the sound carried clearly through the morning. He looked at the exhausted faces, the limp bodies. Imperceptibly he shook his head. Only his wife saw and understood. She took his hand and squeezed it, and he was squeezing back when he heard, also distantly, sirens. But now they were all pushing back from the table, finished, and Bubbles rose slowly to shake with and embrace each one. He knew they would not do this again, ever. (247)

Celebration and loss, a whole complex of emotions and ideas, coalesce in *The Junior Bachelor Society*. The novel speaks more eloquently than any other work by John Williams about the enduring strengths and bonds of men and women who have carved their own lives out of a shared tradition. The novel *is* a celebration: the Bachelors can still assert themselves and, in a very real sense, win the world.

Chapter Eight
Getting to Shore: *!Click Song*

In *The Junior Bachelor Society*, John Williams had given ex
plicit attention for the first time in his fiction to men and
women in middle age, calculating the common ground between their lives and his own. Age and memory motivate
Williams and the Bachelors as they move beyond their fiftieth
years. Both the author and his characters seem concerned
less with world affairs or ideologies than with the dialectic
of personal history and social events. For Williams, trans-
muting facets of his life through the lives of several characters,
there had been a perceptible shift from the major historical
and political issues that once had motivated his protagonists
to the more intimate social consciousness shared by the
Bachelors. Yet it was precisely through the impressive panorama of personalities in *The Junior Bachelor Society* that
Williams would uncover new territory as well as return to
old in his next novel.

Having reconstituted parts of his life in the Bachelors,
Williams was now ready for the fullest and most serious exploration of his life through fiction. The vehicle for this exploration would take him almost seven years to complete.
No longer content to fragment or disperse his own life
through various characters in his fiction, he felt that it was
time to present one protagonist who would literally get
beneath his own skin. In *!Click Song* (1982), a long and
magnificent retrospective, part autobiography and part fiction, John Williams comes to terms completely with the
great idea of self in the modern world.

Organized into a prologue and three major sections, *!Click Song* is the first-person chronicle of Cato Caldwell Douglass, a protagonist who is as corporeal and complete as the author himself, but who is also a representative and highly symbolic figure. Douglass, as his richly allusive first and last names suggest, is a man out of history and shaped by it. He is the stuff of legend and cross-cultural myth, a secular version of Captain Blackman. But before he is any of these things, Cato is a black man, an artist, a husband and father, a walker in the city, a peripatetic man who functions as historical eye. Using a variety of structural prisms and multiple time frames that are far more complex than any plot forms in his previous fiction, Williams explores through his fictional doppelgänger the manifold dimensions of self. At the center of *!Click Song* is contemporary man in perpetual crisis and constant motion, seeking always a special recognition, harmony, and peace.

Autobiography and Fiction

Through his protagonist in *!Click Song*, Williams offers a dramatized and fictionalized version of himself as an artist in America. Moving backward and ahead of a continually progressing present time, using these time shifts to transcribe an existence as rich and yet as elusive as memory itself, the author presents Cato Douglass as a mirror image. Through Cato we can trace the broad outlines of Williams's own history: as an artist in New York, and his perennial battles with publishers, editors, and agents; his travels; his involvement in the political struggles of the 1960s and 1970s; his career in higher education. Anyone familiar with the contours of Williams's life will recognize correspondences in the narrative skein of *!Click Song*.

By superimposing these aspects on the protagonist in the novel, Williams consciously creates autobiographical fiction that permits him both to re-create and to invent facts. Nevertheless, the novel persistently draws strength from the prime objective of pure autobiography—the need to present the truth about the self. Moreover, if Dr. Johnson was correct in observing that the writer of autobiography must be like the historian in "knowledge of the truth," then what we can trace in *!Click Song* is the effort of the author to create a true self beyond the myriad and conflicting currents that seemingly operate to atomize individual identity in the modern world. Of course, the fictional mode permits Williams to transmute the truth, to prevent its correlation with the bland and prosaic realities of life and events. Instead of singular objectivity or a simple chronological account, Williams offers a fictionalized version of his life that is colored inevitably by esthetic bias. For we detect in the beginning of the narrative those ingredients that constitute its ending. Cato Caldwell Douglass is not simply John Williams, but instead a representative figure set in striking relief. He is a man and an artist contending with darkness and potential defeat, a strong but battered swimmer who, as Williams writes late in the novel, is trying to get to shore.

As writer-narrator, Cato functions as a protagonist who can reflect the author's views, rehearse the author's life from an omniscient first-person perspective, and review contemporary history as an almost personal parable. To apply Julius Lester's phrase, Williams is adept at presenting history as personal experience. In this context, what is autobiographical fact and what is fictional invention or artifice is a question that does not confuse esthetic response but rather enhances it, illuminating the manner in which experience always interweaves with fiction to produce art. It is as if we are in touch with the author's life and with Cato's, and through them with the lives of most artists in America. With both the factual author and the fictional author, we are brought closer to an understanding of a society that should have nurtured them, but more typically, made it difficult for them to survive.

What emerges from *!Click Song*, then, is an author and protagonist locked in mortal combat. They enact their drama against a backdrop of social conflict and historical confusion. The author seeks through his protagonist a perspective, one that must be honest and bearable, to measure the potentially tragic interplay of character in a hostile or troublesome world. Cato, more than any other character since Max Reddick, forces Williams to confront and to objectify his own life, but from the twin vantage points of middle age and a different decade. Nevertheless, the basic tensions haunting the author of *The Man Who Cried I Am* and *!Click Song* have the same urgency for the author. Williams acknowledges:

As with *The Man Who Cried I Am*, I had reached another point in my life where I felt the urgent need to say or at least try to say something that has meaning, something that supports the good I have been taught, frames out the good people I know and have met and will, I hope, continue to meet. I look around and see where this one kicked off, that one; I look at Lori's [Williams's wife] mother in her nursing home; I think of my mother briskly plodding ahead, planning with infinite detail matters concerning her own memorial service and cremation (ashes to be buried in Worcester); I see people in those not-so-high places refusing to use any intelligence in their dealings with each other or with other governments; I see almost everyone abdicating even individual responsibility; I see people bereft of vision, of hope, and it is all reflected in the way we behave with each other. I wanted to say that I am not like that; those close to me are not like that, or if I see those tendencies in those close to me, I worry.[1]

The statement reflects both the private emotion and the public perceptions that Williams would weave beautifully into the complex canvas of the novel, and it also hints at the range of characters and concerns that would be involved. His declaration reveals the same preoccupation with last things that typified *The Man Who Cried I Am*. With *!Click Song*, however, the stance toward his own mortality has been refined, perfected, transformed—made clear and positive rather than a bleak certainty. The author and his character stand together, vulnerable figures who remain committed as men and artists to the powerful ability, through words and deeds, to articulate and resolve events.

The pattern of articulation and resolution that Williams develops in *!Click Song* has at its core the unassailably unique role of the black artist in America. This thematic centering permits Williams to range shrewdly and elaborately over broader typologies and myths in an attempt to convey the truth of black experience to a general audience. Truth here begins with the language of black artists and black people—the !click song that dominates as a motif in the novel.[2] It is language that is essentially inimitable by white people. It relates not only to the question of truth and identity but also to the question of who or what ultimately controls social forms and has power over history. The two quotations at the start of the novel suggest this deep thematic relevance:

These . . . are amongst the oldest sounds in language.

Gerald Massey

In my native village . . . there is a song we always sing . . . it's called The Click Song by the English because they cannot say !Click !Clock !Cwlung

Miriam Makeba

If, as Massey in *A Book of Beginnings* asserts, the !click sound is one of the oldest in the language, then it becomes a mark of cultural and historical identity. Moreover, the inability of white people to utter the sound conveys a diminished capacity to deal with origins and with the truth. "I think," Williams observes, "that what I was trying to deal with in part was the absolute loss of value and belief in the spoken word, in the language. I've researched the !click. It is very old. Predynastic Egyptians may have used it. Moses, the man with the strange tongue, may have been a clicker." The !click reinforces revelation of private identity and racial self. Its absence suggests the bankruptcy of language and cultural exhaustion. These antithetical perspectives on the word permit Williams to position the subjective life of the black artist against the broader sociohistorical world that would deny him a voice. Cato Caldwell Douglass, a clicker, erects his own web of words, a distinctive variety of discourse asserting his identity in a society that thrives on the corruption of language.

The language of the ruling class has the power to destabilize and annihilate subjective awareness. This power of language to destroy or simply not to make sense is underscored on the first page of Williams's prologue, entitled "The Cusp." Here the narrator, lunching with his editor, Maureen Gullian, at an East Side restaurant, tries to decipher the words, which strike him as babel: "*Yat, yat yot.*"[3] The time is the late 1970s and Gullian's company, Twentieth Century Forum, has published Cato's last four novels. His new novel, *Unmarked Graves*, never will be published by Twentieth Century Forum, but this knowledge is withheld from readers until much later in the novel. The conversation shifts from Maureen's indecipherable observations on the new novel to her announcement to Cato that earlier in the day an old friend of his, Paul Cummings, had committed suicide. Cato is stunned by the news, for he and Paul had known each other for thirty years, and although they had drifted apart after Paul's success as a "Jewish" novelist, Cato senses in the suicide premonitions of his own mortality. The shock of Paul's death forces Cato to engage in a very special act of recovery—the retrieval of the shards and fragments of his life and those lives that have touched him. This is the force that motivates his autobiography and testament.

"The Cusp" is the cutting edge of *!Click Song*, the sharp recognition of death that each self carries in its passage. To confront death is to constitute consciousness in all its permutations. Thus the highly concentrated five-page prologue offers images of death as a leitmotif: the title of Cato's new novel; the suicide of Paul; reference to the suicide of Ross Lockridge, author of *Raintree County*; allusion to Hamlet's soliloquy; the death five years earlier of Sandra Queensbury, who had introduced Cato to the politics, sexual and otherwise, of the publishing world. At the age of fifty-five, Cato himself had been moving in the shadow of death, preoccupied with "this business of dying" (8).

While offering a purview of death, the prologue also creates a conjunction of past, present, and future events that signals the structure of the entire novel. Speaking of his decision to call the prologue "The Cusp," Williams states:

In this instance where the tangents of past and present are curving to coincide with the events to come. They say that all things have Beginnings (of the novel, of the relationship with Paul), Middles where you actually have one foot in the past and the other in the present, where, even, other events occur or are consolidated or ended because they're only parts of the whole, and Endings where the resolution that people do need each other (Allis [Cato's wife] after the daymare, sitting in the living room, Cato relieved to be alive, pleased to hear the sound of her pen scratching out its poetry) is finally set.

We find in "The Cusp" the three major parts of the novel— Beginnings, Middles, Endings—that mediate and orchestrate the stages and interstices in the history of the self as it wages a struggle for wholeness.

This struggle for wholeness, witnessed in all parts of the novel and in the fluid episodes that move back and forth over a broad temporal spectrum, is basically a battle to achieve a personal, artistic, and (in the largest and most subtle sense) political identity. Success within the system that Williams depicts depends on more than the talent and accomplishments of the artist. Rather it depends on acts of resistance, political acts springing from a keen awareness and understanding of the modes of exploitation that any culture can activate against an individual or group. Cato differs from Max Reddick and other characters of Williams's second phase in his far subtler recognition that resistance and indeed moral responsibility must be daily centers of existence, especially for the black artist. "I think," states Williams, "*!Click Song* is in a more solidly historical sense more political than *The Man* [*Who Cried I Am*]. Direct political action in fiction requires a greater historical knowledge, such as the extent of cultural theft, such as the machinations behind 'making it.'"

Historical knowledge for Williams is still predicated, as it was for DuBois in 1900, on recognition of the color line as the critical problem of the twentieth century. In the second half of the century the problem, however, at least in America, shifts from the need literally to survive in a world predetermined by oppressive history, to retain identity and integrity in a society that ostensibly bends the color line, but only to absorb individuality, neutralize it, and render it malleable. From *Native Son*, to *Invisible Man*, to *The Man Who Cried I Am*, we see in the titles of these seminal novels the powerful need to assert a historical self. With *!Click Song*, Cato more than earlier memorable protagonists has moved beyond the veil, living more in the white world than the black. For one thing, his interracial marriage to Allis serves to mediate between these worlds, although Allis's Jewish heritage forces a new set of historical imperatives on him. For another, Cato early in his adult life elects to be a writer in New York, thereby entering the beast through its brain; for the literary establishment, traditionally a bastion of white power and the most unforgiving of professions, will test Cato's capacity for both personal and artistic survival.

"Beginnings"

"Beginnings," the first and longest section of *!Click Song*, runs at the primary narrative level from World War II through the first Kennedy assassination, ending with the publication of Cato's novel in 1964. Cato is in his early twenties when he meets Paul Cummings in a university writing class that both are attending with financial aid from the GI Bill of Rights. They mature in the second half of the twentieth century, their careers traced like trajectories—one higher than the other in terms of success if not talent—across the American literary landscape. Yet the twenty chapters constituting "Beginnings" do not proceed in strictly chronological fashion. Time and events are as fluid as human consciousness itself.

The essential compositional problem for Williams was to discover a form in which the human and artistic predicament could be articulated in as complete and integrated a manner as possible. To accomplish this objective, he turns the primary narrative in *!Click Song*, which moves through historical time, upon itself. The narrative thus moves back in time and also flashes ahead, even past Paul's funeral. This narrative process turns Cato the narrator into a uniquely omniscient "I." Cato is engaged in an intense meditation and self-expressive act, retelling and elaborating his life and recreating also the lives of individuals who have informed his existence. To discover the self and its relationship to the world, Cato must (as Ellison declares of his protagonist in a similar context) discover that "the end is in the beginning and lies far ahead."

In the first section, we witness beginnings, watch middles unfold, and anticipate ends. Cato must both discover and recover a life, and to this end he ranges over personal existence, proximate lives, history, and culture in order to establish those ontological connections that ultimately will yield meaning to him. Of all Williams's previous novels, only the first, *One For New York*, had been cast in the first person, and that had been a straightforward, deliberately restricted, naturalistic account of a young aspiring artist struggling to survive in the city of dreams. The distance Williams has come as a novelist in the 1980s can be measured in part by the scope and method of *!Click Song*. Williams observes:

The use of the first-person here was for me an exercise, an attempt to avoid the usual, though I knew everyone would believe like hell that this is straightforward autobiography. . . . I wanted to write it because I do believe that books should *say* and *be* objects of importance, even in a society where more and more they are being handled like toilet paper. It took me about seven years, and there were several internal revisions; that is sectional revisions, at times and then tapping back on the beginning. I knew it was going to be complex, yet I also believe that complexity, if it exists, is merely another way of looking at or handling basics.

He creates a complex form of fiction in order to re-create self-consciousness, that most basic issue of human identity.

In "Beginnings" and subsequent sections of *!Click Song*, Williams creates a community of identities framed largely by common interests and roles in the American literary establishment. The novel *is* about American artists. In fact, Williams originally called his novel "Photo by Jill Krementz," a title that did not appeal to editors. What preoccupies Williams is the universe of writers and the "hoopla" that goes with the creation of their success. Basically, he monitors both success for writers like Paul Cummings, who learns to exploit his Jewish identity, and typically the denial of success to black artists. All writers share common dilemmas. Paul, for example, passes through numerous relationships with women and broken marriages, while Cato's first marriage to Catherine (Williams makes little effort to conceal the autobiographical connection here) will also founder, not for the absence of love but on the inability of Catherine to support her husband's desire to be a writer. Both Paul and Cato are also conditioned by racial and cultural backgrounds, although Paul first sublimates his origin and then exploits it. "In trying to detail what America has done to its writers," observes Williams, "I tried to use Paul as an example of how, say, Jewish writers moved (or were allowed to move) from writing of the 'Jewish Experience'—Sholem Asch, Henry Roth, etc.—to the tenuous description of the 'American Experience,' Kantor, early Robbins, even early Mailer, back to the now acceptable, though

in a different time warp, 'New Jewish Experience,' which
has an acceptability never proferred to black writers." In this
context, we see Paul and Cato existing in a binary relationship to the literary world and to American culture. They
both embark on their careers in the early 1950s, Cato with
the greater talent, but Paul reaping the greater success,
ultimately winning the National Book Award for his own
novel on the black experience and enjoying celebrity status.

   Even before he is a Jewish writer, Paul is a white writer,
and thus he does not suffer the cultural containment visited
on Cato by the literary establishment. Cato's first agent, Alex
Samuels, who has also handled such unknown Jewish writers
as Joseph Heller and Bruce Jay Friedman, states the issue suc-
cinctly without comprehending the latent racism in his
remark: "You're going to be the greatest Negro writer in
history" (62). To be trapped in race, to be forced to be
representative of racial consciousness and of the "race problem," is ultimately to be consigned to a literary ghetto. This
is the diminished and extreme fates of the alcoholic Leonard
Blue Sky; of Ike Plunkett, lost to drugs; and of Amos
Bookbinder, token black editor whose wife kills their
children and herself. It was the actual fate of many of the
historical figures to whom Williams alludes in the novel—
Richard Wright, Charlie Parker, Sidney Bechet, and count-
less others railroaded on the "Chitlinswitch Special" (87).
Staring at the still undecorated walls of his first New York
City apartment, Cato at the outset of his odyssey as a writer
knows that he will be a black artist butting his head against
the white barricades of American culture: "I stared at one of
the walls; I thought of running at it full speed, head down, as
if to gut Nagurski, Grange, and Harmon in one, and split my
dolichocephalic head in all its Negroid length right in its
center, to leave trails and splatters of red blood and yellow-
gray brains and pink bone and black skin and have
thereupon, a Pollock or a Middleton" (65). This rage arising
from self-awareness of imposed cultural restraints assumes
suicidal proportions for Cato early in the novel, ultimately
blending with several interlocking motifs of destruction and
creativity, life and death wishes, beginnings and endings.
Whereas Paul succumbs to an inauthentic existence, Cato
struggles toward a sustaining sense of self as well as a viable

place in the world. This is the tale that he wants to tell, the primal motivation for it, the contest between annihilation and affirmation.

In his passage as an individual and writer struggling toward a conception of selfhood in the world, Cato encounters figures who are guides, impediments, mirror images, and nurturing agents. The vast majority of these individuals are writers, artists, agents, editors, and publishers. They include Glenn, the son by his first wife; another son Alejo, who is the product of a short season's relationship with a woman Cato had known in Spain; and Allis herself, who returns to poetry writing after a long hiatus. As with the primary relationship between Cato and Paul, many of these figures cross and recross each other's lives, often over a period of decades. Williams creates an intricate narrative structure to convey this sense of lives converging, diverging, and coming together again in altered forms. Thus even as the primary narrative advances through the stages in Cato's adult life, moving typically from season to season or year to year, Williams in a skillful experimental manner interweaves past, present, and future, often juxtaposing elements or providing information to clarify relationships or events. Typical of this method is the eighth chapter of "Beginnings," primarily a jump in time from the narrative tracing of Cato's early career to the funeral for Paul. The funeral itself incarnates the myth or chronicle of life and death, both of the individual and the artist. Williams also uses this symbolic event, rich in Jewish typologies, to place Paul's death against his first success, to permit Cato to reflect on Allis's own Jewish background and their interracial marriage, to consider his role as a father bringing up sons in a potentially hostile world, and to observe several old friends who have assembled at the funeral, figures from the galaxy of characters who populate the novel. Death is the primal force from the prologue to the end, inducing Cato to reconstruct his own life from the center of dissolution. Williams also must enter this flux at the deepest level of his being in order to locate meaning, value, and the possibility of growth.

Cato's narrative, then, is an act of personal survival, an effort to construct in language a testament to one's desire for life even in the shadow of numerous deaths—Paul, Cato's parents, Jolene Bookbinder and her children, Allis's father, Alejo and his girlfriend who are exterminated by Spanish fascists, more. These deaths, notably those involving black artists, are rarely noble; instead they are self-destructive acts triggered by an avenging literary culture. Thus Leonard Blue Sky, part black and part Native American, is the personification of the minority artist marked for annihilation. He dies on a cold winter night on Lower Broadway, his urine-stained trousers hardened to ice: ". . . the khaki-clad sanitationmen, who daily find parts of bodies and other debris of our time on their jaundiced routes, found him as the sun broke through a cloudy sky over Wall Street and blackened Trinity Church, and chopped him loose" (121). This human universe of lost souls forces Cato to offer a meditation on dying and to scrutinize the very real possibility of his own extinction.

The "autobiography" of Cato Caldwell Douglass, this pilgrim in America, is concurrently an effort to reclaim the individual self from annihilation, to assert one's rightful stature as an artist who refuses to be destroyed, to resist "cultural theft," and to rebel against historical fatality. Cato's inner changes are measured against his discoveries of and immersion in the conflicts of the outer world. Toward the end of the first part, Cato strikes off in 1963 with Mark Medoff to do a television series on the civil rights movement—a journey based on Williams's own explorations that he recorded in *This Is My Country Too*. Cato already has discovered the "machinations" of the literary world but needs a deeper education in historical and political realities. Political consciousness is forged in the violence of the civil rights movement, the trip Cato takes to Africa to film another documentary, the march on Washington, the Kennedy assassination—a rush of events telescoped in the last chapters of "Beginnings." Under the pressure of national and world events, as well as the changing pattern of literary events, an older Cato, the figure who assumes control of the total narrative, traces the movement of a younger consciousness toward the middle stage in his life. This stage corresponds to the central section of the novel, and is signaled by the movement of Cato and Allis from their apartment in Greenwich Village to a large unit on the upper West Side.

"Middles"

The second part of *!Click Song*, entitled "Middles" and consisting of fifteen chapters, is shorter than the first part and less complex in its narrative tapestry. Although Williams continues to telescope both past and future into the present—now the middle—of Cato's life and career, a period running from 1964 to roughly 1971, he concentrates more on chronological events that map the intersections of history with Cato's personal life as husband, father, and author. The section begins with the publication of Cato's third novel, *The Hyskos Journals*, which is about societal and historical decline caused by internal pressures, and a book reviewers do not understand. Concurrently, Paul embraces his Jewishness in *Burnt Offerings*, becoming Kaminsky Cummings and a celebrity in the process. "Middles" ends with controversy over a posthumous award that the Center for Black Arts and Letters wants to give to George Jackson, with Attica, and with Cato's intensifying nightmares; and Paul wins the National Book Award for *Isaiah's Odyssey*, a novel about a black man. After Paul's exploitation of the black theme (Williams might very well have had in mind William Styron and *The Confessions of Nat Turner*, although he declares that Paul is actually a composite of novelists he has known), Cato will never see him again. The section deals with the convergence of lives and events, and with divergences as well.

As writers and public figures, both Cato and Paul are in the "groove of history," as Ellison terms it in *Invisible Man*. Paul, however, attempts to exploit race and history to further his career in the turbulent 1960s; while Cato attempts to analyze history from within, as an individual who lives constantly through history and its dialectical tensions. His marriage to Allis and the birth of their son Mack, whose first five years span the chapters in this section of the novel, enable Cato to mediate many of the personal conflicts in the black and white worlds, and to develop loyalties, quite literally of flesh and blood, that defy race. At the same time, he is forced to deal with racial conflict in his own family, for Glenn, now eighteen and a student at Antioch, has become a militant who is openly hostile to Allis and the white world generally.

Glenn's hostility has been forged in the revolution of the decade. While demonstrating the ways in which historical tensions impinge on ordinary lives, Williams refines and humanizes the depiction of personalities caught in these conflicts. Allis and Glenn are not abstractions or simplified embodiments of ideas and attitudes. They are parts of the same family, tied to Cato, and the patience and love of Allis, as well as Glenn's ability to transcend anger are signs of family strength.

Strength, growth, artistic integrity, family unity: all are painful objectives in the fierce political and cultural conditions of the 1960s. While Cato's "political" novels of the period, *The Hyskos Journals*, *Circles Around Saturn*, *The War Has Already Begun*, are received politely by reviewers, it is clear that the political edge of black writing has only transitory acceptance within the literary establishment. Williams's extended commentary in all sections of the novel on the vagaries and vices of the publishing world, an exposé in which he uses both actual examples and fictionalized events, develops by cumulative weight into one of the most forceful indictments of institutional racism in contemporary fiction. The publishing world is bleak, exploitative, and ugly. Maude Tozer, for one, a powerful book reviewer, would have Cato sleep with her in exchange for a favorable article, a blandishment that he rejects. In fact, retaining sexual integrity is a major hurdle for the denizens of this artistic universe; sexual exploitation is a potent weapon of this professional world. Cato encounters the same problem in academic life, where he succumbs to the sexual politics of a student, Raffy Joplin (who as the daughter of Ralph Jr. serves as the latest link in the chronicle of the Joplin family), knowing that it represents a setback in his constant task to preserve artistic integrity and save himself. Cato ages only a few years in the second part of *!Click Song*, but in keeping with the cataclysmic events governing the period and the narrative—Vietnam, the assassinations of Martin Luther King, Jr., and Robert Kennedy, the death of George Jackson, the massacre at Attica—he seems to be involved in a protracted and deepening struggle to free himself from the destructive forces threatening his family and himself.

Throughout the novel, these forces assume cultural and historical forms that have the capacity to turn existence into a nightmare for individuals. Mr. Storto, the owner of the building and apartment in which Cato lives when he first comes to New York, and an enduring friend of Cato and Allis, has such unnerving nightmares of his World War I experiences that he can only sleep in the daytime. Similarly, Cato's nightmares, which grow in intensity as the protagonist, moving into middle age, is affected by events, are emblems of his existential and historical plight. When, at the end of the second section, Cato dreams of himself as a combat soldier trapped in a jungle that transforms itself into a "dark corridor" and a "maze," he resembles that type of protagonist, depicted vividly in *Invisible Man*, who is kept racing by events. Struggling toward the light, Cato in his nightmare realizes that he is "racing against time. I am shouting and cursing as loud as I can; my shoes, barely touching the surface, make booming sounds" (286). Cato's nightmares are signs that he does not have mental and emotional peace, or even artistic and cultural freedom. His dreams are atavistic, connecting him with the black experience from pre-Dynastic Egyptian times to the present. The invisible but "malevolent" force that impels him through the mazes of his nightmares, tantamount to the beast of a dominant culture on a world scale, is a hostile element that must be fought and subdued.

"Endings"

At the outset of the final part of the novel, "Endings," Cato is on the verge not of reclaiming his life but of losing it. "Endings" is a richly figurative and paradoxical section, containing events that touch on actual deaths, suicides, separations and dissolutions. It traces literary setbacks for Cato and all black artists in the 1970s. It explores cultural demise. Only at the end of the section and the novel, following suicidal doubt and travail, does the light beckoning Cato at the end of the novel seem to offer solace from the nightmare of self trapped by history. Allis's father, who had never reconciled himself to her marriage to Cato, dies at the start of the section. This precipitates a crisis for Allis, who leaves Cato temporarily, and returns to discover that Cato is close to breakdown under personal, professional, and professorial pressures. "Something was wrong with me," surmises Cato, "but I did not know what" (310). Trapped as a "showpiece nigger" at a branch of the public university in New York (a ruthless critique of Williams's experience as a distinguished professor at the City University of New York), Cato finds his "state" worsening under the pressure of an artificial world and an inauthentic existence. He imagines that things are burning—counterpart to a soul on fire and a career in flames. *Unmarked Graves*, the novel that he begins and completes in this section, harbors in its title the sign of Cato's despair. Cato Caldwell Douglass turns fifty in the autumn of 1975 and he, like America, seems to be falling apart.

Williams paradoxically links Cato's sufferings—among them the disappearance and probable death of Alejo, the eclipse of his career by other ethnic fads, dissatisfaction with academic life—to the rebirth of consciousness. Driven almost to suicide, Cato learns that all forms of oppression derive from a dominant culture that is aggressive, highly exploitative, and false. That Falangists have killed his son, that major museums mislabel holdings in order to submerge non-Western culture, and that computers determine whether or not a writer is marketable are not unrelated phenomena; they are historically related, cohering under a tradition of political domination. The cards that Cato starts to hand out to visitors at the Museum of Natural History and at the special Tut exhibit at the Metropolitan Museum of Art are tantamount to a declaration of political resistance—warfare against cultural exploitation. The cards, written in Latin, declare: "Look at the sign. See the proof, the argument collapses. The truth is great and will prevail." Williams takes both Fanon's and Ishmael Reed's concept of cultural theft a step further in *!Click Song* by accurately transcribing the distortions that major museums commit in submerging or obliterating traces of black history and culture. Cato, shuttling from museum to museum distributing his subversive cards, is a seriocomic figure at this stage of the novel, a guerrilla whose mission—the restoration of black culture—is ultimately very serious. Cato knows that in the late 1970s the cultural establishment is not "doing anything black," as an old friend (now gone Hollywood) tells him. If this is the case, then Cato must engage in both overt and covert warfare to free himself from the structures and institutions of historical and cultural oppression.

By the end of *!Click Song*, Cato is much more than the simple autobiographical incarnation of John Williams. (For one thing, Williams has never suffered from nightmares; nor does he have a Spanish son.) The author transmutes through Cato the representative life of the black artist, which is the most distinctive subject of the novel. "We have all traveled essentially the same road," Williams has observed, "met the same barriers, had some of the same experiences. This adds up to a much bigger item than just my life. It is simply that, wherever we turn, on whatever level we manage to climb up to, there waiting is simply another kind of racism." Even at the deepest level of the subconscious life—in Cato's dreams that pit him against God in a game of eight-ball—existence is defined by the contours of racism. For the older Cato of "Endings," racism is more subtle than in earlier times, but more virulent perhaps because of its refined edge. When a computer with the acronym BOOK can relegate black writers' manuscripts to oblivion by controlling the variables, the potency of a dominant culture assumes technological precision, the anonymity of a ruthless machine.

The last two chapters of *!Click Song* are both a lamentation for a lost world of possibilities and an affirmation of one man's life—an author who has searched for and located his character and who has got him to shore. There is in these chapters a cumulative lyrical sadness for everything that has been lost, not the least of which is any hope for the city. At one point, Cato offers an urban meditation:

When I was a young man and had first come to New York, I loved, yes loved, walking around midtown, still emptying of people and slowly refilling with the dinner and theatre crowds, gliding (I told myself) between those great architecturally insane structures all lighted for the silent armies of cleaning people who nightly just appeared, pails, mops and brooms in hand. Although fractured then as

now by race and class, there was at that time an ambience that spoke
of greater possibilities. Like so much else, that is now gone. (422)

The urban world has lost its softer contours of class and
caste, replaced by a fiercely cannibalistic violence. In a compressed, tortured moment of violence, Cato, resisting angrily,
is beaten senseless by three young toughs on a subway train.
He sees "half a millenia, maybe all out of history," (422) in
the eyes of one of these young assailants, the mark that the
war has already begun. This is a diminished and deranged
world, destructiveness consuming and self-consuming, with
the old strategems of power and manipulation also as strong
as ever. For although Amos's firm will accept *Unmarked
Graves*, it will do so only on Amos's agreement that he will
resign. Listening to Miles Davis playing "Solea," Cato and
Amos, whose relationship down the years in New York is
brilliantly evoked by Williams, know the *tired* blues in their
own bones. But they also hear in the music that they listen to
in a New York bar, the continual urge to affront and assault
the culture that has caused their weariness.

Cato's final nightmare, in which he dreams his death at the
hands of New York cops who have come to arrest him for
his museum capers, signifies the end of his self-destructive
tendencies. He awakens to the peaceful sound of Allis's voice
and pen creating poetry. In her poem is the tone and tenor of
their relationship, and also the bedrock of all that is affirmative in their lives:

> Wracked, soul in traction and
> sprawled, a wind-downed scarecrow
> among bound words heaped as though
> for burning, bound words blown of
> meaning, his sons absent, his love of
> them leaking redly in tiny tunnels
> crafted by an ancient, awful alchemy,
> is my husband, snared by their hate,
> my love. He speaks in clicks. I know
> his tongue. I !click back to him.
> I know the language. It is ours. (430)

The air on waking is "strangely sharp and wonderfully
sweet" for Cato. The violence of the past twenty-four hours,

replicated and intensified by the nightmare, has served as catharsis. His !click song is testament to all that is valuable in life—allegiance to family and friends, to artistic craft, and to the perpetual effort to shape a world better than he has found it.

The Career

"Autobiographical fiction," John Williams observes, "must radiate from self through the universe. It's only good for that. One must have the sense, even as one must certainly write for one's self, that out there in the silent, tho' busy cosmos, there are others as happy, as bitter, as aware as you think yourself to be." Although the passage of Cato Caldwell Douglass parallels the career of the author, it is the powerful and revealing journey of the black writer—indeed all artists—in America. Trapped within history and culture, Cato must evolve new critical perspectives on the American experience in order to maintain identity, adhere to a viable code of values, prosper, and survive. The interplay of creative and destructive forces in Cato's life and the personal revelations this tension fosters provide the dramatic fabric for a novel that explores and recapitulates many of the significant themes that John Williams has investigated throughout his career.

!Click Song grows from the author's personal experiences, but the novel projects a vision of representative people contending with fundamental forces that persistently shape American society. From the fluid, complex, and remarkable narrative perspective, both protagonist and author erect a coherent sense of self—a meaningful context in which they can live. The novel is unique in terms of Williams's work and original in its presentation of both the subjective life and a persistent analysis of American culture. It is a personal epic, finely designed in technique and plot, deft in stylistic execution, and great in subject.

Chapter Nine
The Territory Ahead

For John Williams, the territory ahead is no longer un-chartered, although it might still hold surprises for him and for his expanding reading public. His personal and artistic worlds can never be apolitical, and thus the fiction of the future will continue to flesh out those points on the literary and historical map that have always been central to his vision: racism, exploitation, and oppression; characters on a collision course with history who seek nevertheless personal and political affirmations. In the meantime, Williams's visibility and prominence as a major writer and interpreter of the American scene continue to evolve slowly. The superlative presentation of a three-part television film based on *The Junior Bachelor Society*, aired in late September of 1981, brought a new dimension of success and recognition to its author. *!Click Song*, released in the spring of 1982, pro-jects new strengths as well as a deeper, softer, and more reflective voice of the mature artist. His play, *Last Flight from Ambo Ber*, first offered in trial production in Boston, breaks new literary ground but is still political and historical in nature, covering a period of more than seventy-five years. He is writing a book on Richard Pryor for the New American Library. Today he is writing poetry again, poems that are longer than those that signaled the start of his career, nar-rative epics embracing the black experience on a world scale. "I like writing poems," Williams confesses, "and hope one day that someone will say, 'To hell with your novels; read us some of your poetry.' These tend to be historical in the sense that they are glimpses of injustices, racial and otherwise, and not unlike my other work." Still at the center of his expanding artistic universe is the novel and Williams's commitment to fiction of consequence. One novel, started in the mid-1970s and set in an Africa that is framed by American interests, is in the vein of direct political fiction that he wants to return to.

John Williams today is as busy as he was at earlier stages in his career when he had to struggle for recognition. From his home and study in Teaneck, New Jersey, a town that suits him well, he devotes time to preparing challenging lessons for his journalism and literature students at the Newark campus of Rutgers University. When he is not preoccupied with classes, he concentrates on literary projects, rereading typed pages from the day before, working from handwritten notes on new material, moving from morning to late afternoon and, if it is going well, working after dinner. His common field of vision remains constant and in keeping with those major writers who, in Williams's words, "struggle through impediments to discover whatever progress we might be able to make, one human to another."

The novels of John Williams, which ultimately will be the measure of his stature as an artist, offer to us what Lionel Trilling termed "our sense of a culture's hum and buzz of implication . . . the whole evanescent context in which explicit statements are made." In both their uniqueness and commonality, the novels draw us together in a web of cultural and historical recognition. Williams wants us to learn something intense and powerful about American life from his work. And the hardships that we uncover in the fiction are balanced by the affirmations—the confirmation that in returning to ourselves and the basic values that make us human, we understand ourselves and the world better. Williams persistently has revealed the worst and tried to confirm the best aspects of our lives in the modern period. This is his constant task, and one that he does not plan to abandon. For the circus is still going on, he declares, the tent never closes.

Notes and References

Chapter One

1. "Career By Accident," *Flashbacks: A Twenty-Year Diary of Article Writing* (Garden City, N.Y., 1974), p. 394.
2. Saunders Redding, "The Negro Writer and American Literature," in *Anger and Beyond: The Negro Writer in the United States*, ed. Herbert Hill (New York: Harper & Row, 1966), p. 3.
3. "Time and Tide: The Roots of Black Awareness," *Flashbacks*, p. 409.
4. "This Is My Country Too," *Flashbacks*, pp. 36–37.
5. Ibid., pp. 37–38.
6. For an amusing account of Williams's trials as a young mathematician see "The Figure Eight," in *The McGraw-Hill Reader*, ed. Gilbert H. Muller (New York: McGraw-Hill, 1982), pp. 18–21.
7. Unpublished autobiographical sketch, 1978, p. 2.
8. Ibid., p. 3.
9. "The Boys From Syracuse," *Present Tense*, 4 (Spring 1977):36.
10. When Williams last saw Doris Schmau in 1967, he asked what she had meant, and she replied that good teachers have a habit of "just knowing."
11. "This Is My Country Too," p. 38.
12. Ibid., p. 39.
13. Autobiographical sketch, p. 6.
14. Ibid., p. 7.
15. Ibid.
16. Ibid., p. 8.
17. A thorough and generally perceptive analysis of this story appears in Peter Freese, "John A. Williams' 'Son in the Afternoon,'" in *The Black American Short Story in the Twentieth Century*, ed. Peter Bruck (Amsterdam, 1977), pp. 141–54.
18. Interview with John Williams, February 2, 1981.
19. See, for example, Paul Pickrell's review in *Harper's*, November 1961, p. 120.

20. For an extensive, well-documented account of this episode, see Blossom Kirschenbaum, "*Prix de Rome*: The Writing Fellowship given by the Academy of Arts and Letters in Conjunction with the American Academy in Rome, 1951–1963," Ph.D. dissertation, Brown University, 1972.

21. Williams's own account of the episode appears in "We Regret to Inform You That," *Flashbacks*, pp. 357–66. This quotation is from a letter in Williams's files.

22. "We Regret to Inform You That," p. 364.

23. Williams, under the Freedom of Information Act, has acquired some of this material.

24. Eric Moon, review of *Sons of Darkness, Sons of Light*, *Library Journal*, 94(15 June 1969):2455.

Chapter Two

1. *Flashbacks*, p. 4.

2. "The Negro in Literature Today," *Ebony*, September 1963, p. 73.

3. Ibid.

4. *Flashbacks*, p. 9.

5. Williams ghost wrote *The Protectors: Our Battle Against The Crime Gangs* (New York, 1964) for Harry T. Anslinger, who was former U.S. Commissioner of Narcotics. He uses the pseudonym "J. Dennis Gregory." As he explains in an interview in Earl A. Cash, *John A. Williams: The Evolution of a Black Writer* (New York, 1975): "*The Protectors* was published in April, 1964. I used a pseudonym—J for John; Dennis for my youngest son; Gregory for my oldest son. I did not feel that I should use my name on this because it is not a novel and because I've never approved of all the methods used by the Narcotics Bureau. The methods I disliked you won't find here except between the lines where I managed to put them. However, and frankly, I had no quarrel with the money it paid; sad, but true" (p. 12).

6. John O'Brien, ed., *Interviews With Black Writers* (New York, 1973), p. 229.

7. "The Literary Ghetto," *Saturday Review*, 20 April 1962, p. 21.

8. Ibid., p. 40.

9. "The Negro in Literature Today," *Ebony*, September 1963), p. 21.

10. Joseph T. Skerrett, Jr., "Novelist in Motion: Interview with John Williams," *Black World* 15(January 1976):67.

11. "Ralph Ellison and *Invisible Man*: Their Place in American Letters," *Black World* 20(December 1970):11.

12. "The Manipulation of History and of Fact," in *William Styron's Nat Turner: Ten Black Writers Respond*, ed. John Henrik Clarke (Boston: Beacon Press, 1968), pp. 45–46.

13. "The Crisis in American Letters," *The Black Scholar* 6(June 1975):67.

14. Ibid., p. 71.

15. "The Survival of Creativity: Writers as Critics of American Society," *LaGuardia Review*, Spring 1977:13.

16. Ibid., p. 15.

17. *The Most Native of Sons: A Biography of Richard Wright* (Garden City, N.Y., 1970), p. 3. Subsequent page references are to this edition.

18. *Africa: Her History, Lands and People*, 3rd ed. (New York, 1969), p. 3. Subsequent page references are to this edition.

19. *The King God Didn't Save* (New York, 1970), p. 17. Subsequent page references are to this edition.

20. See Richard J. Neuhaus, "Martin Luther King's Second Assassination," *New York Review of Books*, 8 October 1970, pp. 45–49.

21. *This Is My Country Too* (New York, 1965), p. 1. Subsequent page references are to this edition.

22. See the series of essays, "Three Negro Families," "The Negro Middle Class," and "The Strongest Negro Institution" in *Flashbacks*, pp. 112–77.

23. "Changing Times in Plains," *Reader's Digest*, July 1977, pp. 133–36.

Chapter Three

1. For a typical discussion of this classification, see Noel Schraufnagel, *From Apology to Protest: The Black American Novel* (Deland, Fla: Everett Edwards, 1973), pp. 147–51.

2. Preface to *Sissie* (Chatham, N.J., 1975). Subsequent page references are to this edition.

3. Writing in *The Souls of Black Folk* (1903), DuBois declared: "One can feel his twoness, an American, a Negro; two souls, two thoughts, two unreconciled strivings; two warring ideals in one dark body."

4. *Flashbacks*, p. 218.

5. For an early discussion of the genre as it relates to *Night Song*, see Ralph J. Gleason, "The Jazz Novel—A Two-Fold Problem," *San Francisco Chronicle*, 5 November 1961, p. 29.

6. *Night Song* (Chatham, N.J., 1961), p. 10. Subsequent page references are to this edition.

7. *Sissie* (Garden City, N.Y., 1969), vii. Subsequent page references are to this edition.

8. Williams apparently uses part of Charlie Parker's psychiatric report to create the report on Ralph. See *Flashbacks*, p. 219.

9. Ralph Ellison, "A Very Stern Discipline," *Harper's*, March 1967, p. 76.

Chapter Four

1. Speaking with Dan Georgakas, "John Williams at 49: An Interview," *Minnesota Review* (Fall 1976), Williams observed: "Styron was certainly better known inside the literary establishment which is where it counts, and there was the obvious business of being a successor to Faulkner. All that helps. My wife believes my novel got good notices, but that was long after it got published. I had an extremely good editor who is now dead. Harry Sions. He expressed fears that Styron's book would catch a lot of attention. He drafted the publicity blurb he wanted Little, Brown to use. I remember one key word he used, blockbuster" (p. 52).

2. *This Is My Country Too*. Summarizing these misgivings about America, he wrote, "I am committed to the search for its true meaning; I hope what I have found is not it" (p. 169).

3. For a probing treatment of the relationship between history and contemporary fiction, see Mas'ud Zavarzadeh, *The Mythopoeic Reality: The Postwar American Nonfiction Novel* (Urbana: University of Illinois Press, 1977).

4. Georg Lukács, *The Historical Novel*, trans. Hannah and Stanley Mitchell (London: Merlin Press, 1962), p. 41.

5. *The Man Who Cried I Am* (Boston, 1967), p. 4. Subsequent page references are to this edition.

6. In the Georgakas interview, Williams noted: "I think that Wright's historical view certainly couldn't help but influence any writer. All they teach in lit classes is *Native Son*. I wonder if they even know his other writings, his stuff on Spain, the Third World, and Africa. In the beginning of *White Man, Listen*, he runs down a whole page of what reads like very good poetry about what happened in the fifteenth, sixteenth, and seventeenth centuries regarding slavery, not just African slavery, but the world picture, the kind of slavery that was part of colonialism. It's just a tremendous historical setting. I'm into that. I think history is a good base for me" (p. 53).

7. Williams's reservations about Martin Luther King, Jr., culminating in his scathing *The King God Didn't Save* (1970), were of long standing, and some of the recent revelations about King's

personal life are touched on in *The Man Who Cried I Am*. Comparing King and Malcolm X through their fictive avatars, he wrote: "Where Durrell employed fanciful imagery and rhetoric, Minister Q preached history, economics, and religion of race relations; he preached a message so harsh it hurt to listen to" (p. 209).

8. In an interview with Earl A. Cash, *John A. Williams*, Williams said: "Actually I could see the times when Max was like myself. Because I had done some work for *Newsweek* in Africa with a specific job in mind to look for a desk in West Africa. I had been down to the Congo and a few other places. I had covered part of the Ethiopian-Somali war for *Newsweek*. But in the main, Chester Himes was my Max. His was the figure I held up pretty much" (p. 153).

9. See Anncliese H. Smith, "A Pain in the Ass: Metaphor in John A. Williams's *The Man Who Cried I Am*," *Studies in Black Literature* 3(1972):25–27.

10. Ronald Walcott, "*The Man Who Cried I Am*: Crying in the Dark," *Studies in Black Literature* 3(1972):29, writes: "Reddick is not a hero in the conventional sense, that is, an active and informing and developing consciousness the outcome of which determines the course of the narrative; rather, he is a necessary and convenient presence through which certain things can be seen and statements made."

11. For an excellent appraisal of Melville as a radical artist, see H. Bruce Franklin, *The Victim as Criminal and Artist* (New York: Oxford University Press, 1978), pp. 31–70.

12. See Robert F. Fleming, "'Playing the Dozens' in the Black Novel," *Studies in Black Literature* 3(1972):23–24.

13. Lukács, *The Historical Novel*, p. 34.

14. See David Henderson, "*The Man Who Cried I Am*: A Critique," in *Black Expression*, ed. Addison Gayle, Jr. (New York, 1969), pp. 370–71.

15. "Backtracking Pioneers," *New York Herald Tribune Book Week*, 7 June 1974, p. 2.

Chapter Five

1. Earl A. Cash, Interview with John Williams, October 25, 1971, *John A. Williams*, pp. 137–38.

2. *Sons of Darkness, Sons of Light* (Boston, 1969), p. 3. Subsequent page references are to this edition.

3. Cash, *John A. Williams*, p. 134.

4. Ibid., p. 138.

5. Noel Schraufnagel, *From Apology to Protest*, p. 192.

Chapter Six

1. Malcom Cowley, *The Literary Situation* (New York: Viking, 1954), p. 34.
2. For a discussion of the genre, see Peter G. Jones, *War and the Novelist* (Columbia: University of Missouri Press, 1976).
3. "Navy Black" is a fragment from one of these projects.
4. Cash, p. 154.
5. *Captain Blackman* (Garden City, N.Y., 1972), p. 14. Subsequent page references are to this edition.
6. Richard Chase, *The American Novel and Its Tradition* (Garden City, N.Y.: Doubleday/Anchor, 1957), p. 13.
7. Georgakas, "John Williams at 49," p. 56.
8. "The Manipulation of History and of Fact," in Clarke, p. 46.
9. "Backtracking Pioneers," *New York Herald Tribune Book Week*, 7 June 1964, p. 2.
10. For a cogent presentation of this problem of historiography see Herbert Butterfield, *Man on His Past: The Study of History and Historical Scholarship* (Cambridge: Cambridge University Press, 1955).
11. Williams even experimented with the possibility of using ghosts to transmit the lessons of history in *Captain Blackman*.
12. Quoted in Martin Esslin, *Brecht: A Choice of Evils* (London: Heinemann, 1973), p. 109.
13. Georgakas, "John Williams at 49," p. 50.

Chapter Seven

1. *Mothersill and the Foxes* (Garden City, N.Y. 1975), p. 24. Subsequent page references are to this edition.
2. *The Junior Bachelor Society* (Garden City, N.Y., 1976), p. 1. Subsequent page references are to this edition.
3. Jacques Ellul, *Violence: Reflections from a Christian Perspective* (New York: Seabury Press, 1969), p. 94.

Chapter Eight

1. Letter from John Williams, November 10, 1981. Subsequent statements by Williams are from this letter.
2. The click motif embodies a variety of meanings in the novel, ranging from the uniqueness of speech and culture to imaginative insight to such purely mechanical but important sounds as the clicking of Cato's typewriter or the clicking of a cop's gun.
3. *!Click Song* (Boston, 1982), p. 3. Subsequent page references are to this edition.

Selected Bibliography

PRIMARY SOURCES

1. Novels

The Angry Ones. New York: Ace Books, 1960; Pocket Books, 1970. (See also *One For New York*.)

Captain Blackman: A Novel. Garden City, N.Y.: Doubleday & Co., 1972; Bantam, 1973.

!Click Song. Boston: Houghton Mifflin Co. 1982.

The Junior Bachelor Society. Garden City, N.Y.: Doubleday & Co., 1976.

The Man Who Cried I Am. Boston: Little, Brown & Co., 1967; New York: New American Library, 1972.

Mothersill and the Foxes. Garden City, N.Y.: Doubleday & Co., 1975.

Night Song. New York: Farrar, Straus & Cudahy, 1961; New York: Pocket Books, 1970; Chatham, N.J.: Chatham Bookseller, 1975.

One For New York. Chatham, N.J.: Chatham Bookseller, 1975. (Originally published as *The Angry Ones*, 1960.)

Sissie. New York: Farrar, Straus & Cudahy, 1963; New York: Anchor Books, 1969; Chatham, N.J.: Chatham Bookseller, 1975.

Sons of Darkness, Sons of Light: A Novel of Some Probability. Boston: Little, Brown & Co., 1969; New York: Pocket Books, 1970.

2. Nonfiction

Africa: Her History, Lands and People. New York: Cooper 1963.

Flashbacks: A Twenty-year Diary of Article Writing. Garden City, N.Y.: Doubleday & Co., 1970. This collects all of Williams's important essays except for those listed below.

The King God Didn't Save: Reflections on the Life and Death of Martin Luther King, Jr. New York: Coward-McCann, 1970; New York, Pocket Books, 1971.

The Most Native of Sons. Garden City, N.Y.: Doubleday & Co.,
     1970.
*The Protectors: The Heroic Story of the Narcotics Agents,
     Citizens and Officials in their Unending, Unsung Battles
     against Organized Crime in America and Abroad.* Cowrit-
     ten by Harry J. Anslinger with J. Dennis Gregory
     (pseudonym for John A. Williams). New York: Farrar, Straus
     & Co., 1964.
This Is My Country Too. New York: New American Library,
     1965; 1966.

3. Short Fiction
"Father and Son." *Negro Digest.* January 1963, pp. 59–60.
"A Good Season." In Woody King, ed., *Black Short Story An-
     thology.* New York: Columbia University Press, 1972, pp.
     107–16.
"Joey's Sled." *Negro Digest.* January 1963, pp. 58–59.
"Navy Black." In John A. Williams, ed., *Beyond the Angry Black.*
     New York: Cooper Square Publishers, 1966, pp. 157–18.
"Son in the Afternoon." In James A. Emanuel and Theodore L.
     Gross, eds., *Dark Symphony.* New York: Free Press, 1968,
     pp. 394–99.

4. Uncollected articles and essays
"Black Publisher, Black Writer: An Impasse." *Black World*
     March 1975, pp. 28–31.
"Black Writers' Views on Literary Lions and Values." *Negro
     Digest.* June 1967, pp. 31–38.
"Changing Times in Plains." *Reader's Digest,* July 1977,
     pp. 133–36.
"The Crisis in American Letters." *Black Scholar* 6 (June 1975):
     67–72.
"Literary Ghetto." *Saturday Review* 2 April 1963, pp. 21, 40.
"The Negro in Literature Today." *Ebony* September 1963,
     pp. 73–76.
"Race, War, and Politics." *Negro Digest* August 1967, pp. 4–9,
     36–47.
"Ralph Ellison and *Invisible Man*: Their Place in American Let-
     ters." *Black World.* December 1970, pp. 10–11.
"The Survival of Creativity: Writers as Critics of American So-
     ciety." *The LaGuardia Review,* Spring 1977, pp. 13–15.
"The Task of the Negro Writer as Artist." *Negro Digest*
     pp. 66–70.

"The United States: A Nice Place to Visit." *Saturday Review*
27 January 1968, pp. 30–31.
"The Way it Is: An Open Letter to an African." *Negro Digest*
September 1965, pp. 22, 28–35.

5. Anthologics (Editor)
Amistad, with Charles F. Harris. New York: Random House,
vol. 1, 1970; vol. 2, 1971.
The Angry Black. New York: Cooper Square, 1962.
Beyond the Angry Black. New York: Lancer Books, 1967.

6. Interviews
Baker, John F. "PW Interviews: John A. Williams." *Publishers
Weekly*, 7 June 1976, pp. 12–13.
Cash, Earl A. "Interviews October 25, 1971 and June 9, 1972."
In Cash, *John A. Williams: The Evolution of a Black
Writer*. New York: Third Press, 1975, pp. 131–62.
Georgakas, Dan. "John Williams at 49: An Interview." *Minnesota
Review* 7 (Fall 1976):56–65.
O'Brien, John. "The Art of John A. Williams: An Interview."
American Scholar 42 (Summer 1973):489–94. Reprinted in
Interviews with Black Writers. New York: Liveright, 1973.
"Seeking a Humanist Level: Interview with John A. Williams."
Arts in Society 10 (Spring-Summer 1973):94–99.
Skerrett, Joseph T., Jr. "Interview with John A. Williams." *Black
World* 25 (January 1976):58–67, 93–97.

SECONDARY SOURCES

1. Book
Cash, Earl A. *John A. Williams: The Evolution of a Black
Writer*. New York: Third Press, 1975, The first full-length
study of Williams's work, covering the important nonfiction and the novels through *Captain Blackman*. Contains a
judicious evaluation of the "black esthetic" as applied to
Williams's major books, and a valuable set of interviews
with Williams conducted by Cash.

2. Articles and chapters of books
Bigsby, C. W. E. *The Second Black Renaissance*. Westport,
Conn.: Greenwood Press, 1980, pp. 154–66 passim,

172–79. Traces Williams's progress as a novelist from "anger over individual suffering" to "growing awareness of historical processes."

Bryant, Jerry H. "John A. Williams: The Political Use of the Novel." *Critique* 16, no. 3 (1975):81–100. Bryant sees Williams at "the center of black fiction" in the 1960s and continuing the tradition of Richard Wright—an effort to express the concerns of black Americans in fictional form. Charges that novels are uneven because he "has expended his talents more on politics than on art." Finds only *The Man Who Cried I Am* to be a blend of "good fiction and good politics."

Burke, William M. "The Resistance of John A. Williams: *The Man Who Cried I Am.*" *Critique* 15 no. 3 (1974):5–14. A useful article in which Burke emphasizes the "circularity" of the novel's plot and the relationship of this structure to the historical traps that ensnare Max Reddick.

Fleming, Robert E. "The Nightmare Level of *The Man Who Cried I Am.*" *Contemporary Literature* 14 (Spring 1973):186–96. The author explores those gothic and grotesque elements in the novel that liberate Williams from "the naturalistic format which for a time seemed the sole metier of the black novelist."

———. "'Playing the Dozens' in the Black Novel." *Studies in Black Literature* 3 (1972):23–24. A brief essay asserting that such activities as playing the dozens expose the "cultural gaps" between white and black audiences. Fleming alludes to Williams's *The Man Who Cried I Am*, Wright's "Big Boy Leaves Home" and *Lawd Today*, and Ellison's *Invisible Man* for literary examples of verbal exchanges rooted in black language and culture.

Foley, Barbara. "History, Fiction and the Ground Between: The Uses of the Documentary Mode in Black Literature." *PMLA* 95 (May 1980):389–403. A provocative theoretical analysis of black American narrative art. Foley asserts that Afro-American writers use factuality "to persuade their readers of the truths proposed in their texts." References to *The Man Who Cried I Am* and *Captain Blackman*.

Freese, Peter. "John A. Williams: 'Son in the Afternoon.'" In Peter Bruck, ed., *The Black American Short Story in the Twentieth Century*. Amsterdam: B. R. Gruner, 1977, pp. 141–56. A careful textual analysis of Williams's story as a compressed study of "racial relations in America."

Gayle, Addison Jr. *The Way of the New World: The Black Novel in America.* Garden City, N.Y.: Doubleday, 1975, pp. 277–88. Williams's novels "evidence a steady progression from protest to assertion, from a feeble optimism to a hard-learned reality." Focuses on the author's talent for historical analysis in *The Man Who Cried I Am* and *Captain Blackman.*

Henderson, David. "*The Man Who Cried I Am*: A Critique." In Addison Gayle, Jr., ed. *Black Expression.* New York: Weybright and Talley, 1969, pp. 365–71. A militant essay, concentrating on the King Alfred Plan in the novel and asserting that black genocide is not as farfetched as Americans might think: "A plan for the extermination of American blacks would not be contrary to American history."

Klotman, Phyllis R. "An Examination of the Black Confidence Man in Two Black Novels: *The Man Who Cried I Am* and *Dem.*" *American Literature* 44 (January 1973):596–611. Williams develops a relatively new fictional character, "the black espionage agent," in *The Man Who Cried I Am.*

Major, Clarence. *The Dark and Feeling: Black American Writers and Their Work.* New York: Third Press, 1974, pp. 85–94. A crisp biographical-critical appreciation of the author, containing useful personal information on Williams.

Schraufnagel, Noel. *From Apology to Protest: The Black American Novel.* Deland, Fla.: Everett/Edwards, 1973, pp. 147–51, 197–92. Surveys Williams's novels of the 1960s, classifying the first three in the tradition of the "apologetic protest novel" and the last two as militant protest."

Smith, Anneliese H. "A Pain in the Ass: Metaphor in John A. Williams' *The Man Who Cried I Am.*" *Studies in Black Literature* 3 (Autumn 1972):25–27. A careful elucidation of the numerous metaphors relating to Max Reddick's rectal cancer that serves as a motif for both the protagonist's terminal condition and the sickness of Western society.

Walcott, Ronald. "The Early Fiction of John A. Williams." *CLA Journal* 16 (December 1972):198–213. Examines the autobiographical elements in Williams's first three works. Treats *The Angry Ones* and *Night Song* as "apprentice works at best" and *Sissie* as Williams's first important novel.

———. "*The Man Who Cried I Am*: Crying in the Dark." *Studies in Black Literature* 3 (Spring 1972):24–32. A survey

of Williams's work during the 1960s. Walcott rightly
perceives Williams's vision shifting from a confident tone
to the "political" conclusion that America is caught in a
destructive "crisis of faith." Thus *The Man Who Cried I
Am* "may be read as the chronicle of Max Reddick's
political education."

Index

169